Feed

A play

Tom Elliott

Samuel French — London
New York - Toronto - Hollywood

© 2000 BY TOM ELLIOTT (BOOK AND LYRICS)

Rights of Performance by Amateurs are controlled by Samuel French Ltd, 52 Fitzroy Street, London W1P 6JR, and they, or their authorized agents, issue licences to amateurs on payment of a fee. **It is an infringement of the Copyright to give any performance or public reading of the play before the fee has been paid and the licence issued.**

The Royalty Fee indicated below is subject to contract and subject to variation at the sole discretion of Samuel French Ltd.

Basic fee for each and every
performance by amateurs   Code M
in the British Isles
(play and music)

The Professional Repertory Rights in this play are controlled by Samuel French Ltd

---

The publication of this play does not imply that it is necessarily available for performance by amateurs or professionals, either in the British Isles or Overseas. Amateurs and professionals considering a production are strongly advised in their own interests to apply to the appropriate agents for written consent before starting rehearsals or booking a theatre or hall.

ISBN 0 573 01760 3

Please see page iv for further copyright information

822

Feed

First performed at the Octagon Theatre. Bolton, on September 10th, 1992, with the following cast of characters:

Harry Troop	Roy Barraclough
Stephanie/Stella Turner	Henrietta Whitsun Jones
Edith/Jessie/BBC Woman	Lesley Nicol

Directed by **Lawrence Till**
Designed by **Penny Fitt**
Lighting by **Jeremy Newman-Roberts**

Musical Director/Keyboards **Carol Donaldson**
Keyboards **Richard Wetherall**

COPYRIGHT INFORMATION

(See also page ii)

This play is fully protected under the Copyright Laws of the British Commonwealth of Nations, the United States of America and all countries of the Berne and Universal Copyright Conventions.

All rights including Stage, Motion Picture, Radio, Television, Public Reading, and Translation into Foreign Languages, are strictly reserved.

No part of this publication may lawfully be reproduced in ANY form or by any means — photocopying, typescript, recording (including video-recording), manuscript, electronic, mechanical, or otherwise—or be transmitted or stored in a retrieval system, without prior permission.

Licences for amateur performances are issued subject to the understanding that it shall be made clear in all advertising matter that the audience will witness an amateur performance; that the names of the authors of the plays shall be included on all programmes; and that the integrity of the authors' work will be preserved.

The Royalty Fee is subject to contract and subject to variation at the sole discretion of Samuel French Ltd.

In Theatres or Halls seating Four Hundred or more the fee will be subject to negotiation.

In Territories Overseas the fee quoted above may not apply. A fee will be quoted on application to our local authorized agent, or if there is no such agent, on application to Samuel French Ltd, London.

VIDEO-RECORDING OF AMATEUR PRODUCTIONS

Please note that the copyright laws governing video-recording are extremely complex and that it should not be assumed that any play may be video-recorded for whatever purpose without first obtaining the permission of the appropriate agents. The fact that a play is published by Samuel French Ltd does not indicate that video rights are available or that Samuel French Ltd controls such rights.

CHARACTERS

Harry Troop, a retired Variety artiste
Stephanie, Troop's nurse, mid-20s
Edith, Troop's daughter, middle-aged

The actress playing Stephanie also plays **Stella Turner**
The actress playing Edith plays **Jessie** and **BBC Woman**

The action of the play takes place in the Havencrest Nursing Home and the various stages and dressing-rooms of Harry Troop's memory

Time: the present

A licence issued by Samuel French Ltd to perform this play does not include permission to use any Incidental music other than that composed by Derek Hilton with lyrics by Tom Elliott. Where the place of performance is already licensed by the PERFORMING RIGHT SOCIETY a return of the music used must be made to them. If the place of performance is not so licensed then application should be made to the Performing Right Society, 29 Berners Street, London W1.

A separate and additional licence from PHONOGRAPHIC PERFORMANCES LTD, 1 Upper James Street, London W1R 3HG is needed whenever commercial recordings are used.

Feed was first performed at the Octagon Theatre, Bolton in 1992. In 1993 it played in repertory with *The Norman Conquests* by Alan Ayckbourn at the Stephen Joseph Theatre, Scarborough. A subsequent 12-week tour opened at the Playhouse Theatre, Liverpool.

Feed was awarded Best New Play at the Manchester Evening News Theatre Awards 1993 where Roy Barraclough won Best Actor. Roy Barraclough was also awarded Best Actor for this play in the Liverpool Echo North West Arts Awards in 1994.

The music for the songs, and the incidental music, by Tom Elliott and Derek Hilton, arranged for two keyboards, is available on hire from Samuel French Ltd. The performance fee for the play includes the use of the music but there will be a small charge for the hire of the score.

ACT I

Dark stage

Music Cue No 1. *Fade up seaside sounds—seagulls crying, pipe organ playing* I Do Like to Be Beside the Seaside. *Mix with audience laughter, then fade up laughter above fading seaside sounds. Hold laughter a moment. Fade laughter to silence. Hold a few seconds*

Spot snaps on Troop, C. *He poses in a natty blazer, monocle, straw hat and cane*

Troop A young ballet dancer called Jake
Lost his codpiece one night in Swan Lake
A lady then said:
"The swan might be dead
But there's plenty of life in the snake!"

Music Cue No 2. *Piano plays vamp till ready as Troop moves* DS *to greet the audience*

Good evening, ladies and gentleman. You are in the company of a true-blue aristocrat. Smythe's the name—Algernon Beckwith-Smythe. Descended from a long line of gartered knights, belted earls, battered fish and crushed olives. The motto on my escutcheon reads "Honour Before Dark"... I usually am if she's willin'! But one mustn't believe all one reads. It says "thirty-six waist" on my under-drawers but there's not much wasted, I can tell you! (*He sings* Deb's Delight)
    You'll see me often out
    In high-class places
    At the races
    Or by the sea

    I have a talent
    For the social graces
    All female faces
    They beam at me

    I suppose it's *savoir-faire*

Ici or anywhere
That has them all declare
That I'm OK.

So when Algie hits the town
You can bet a half-a-crown
That the Deb's Delight
Will have his wicked way!

Music vamps softly on... Troop moves laterally in the spot

A little terpsichorean magic here now, ladies and gentlemen... Watch the feet. No hidden extras. Available for cash at any retail branch of Freeman, Hardy & Willis... So this man said to me, he said... (*He begins a slow dance turn*) Hang on, I'll be back... (*He completes the turn*) He said: "My dog can't tell whisky from water." I said, "Is it blind?" He said, "Yes—most of the time". (*He indicates his feet to an imaginary lady in front stalls*) Fascinating, isn't it? You know what they say about a man's size in shoes, Madam... Smile if you've heard it. (*He reacts to the audience*) Heard it? Blimey, she's proved it! (*He sings* Deb's Delight)

    At a party yesterday
    I went all stallion
    On gin Italian
    And iced champagne

    I had a glass
    With a classy lass with a sari on
    Oh what a carry-on!
    An Eastern flame.

    In her hair there was a rose
    A jewel in her nose
    And an air of such repose
    My heart took flight.

    And as she sipped on her gin
    I said "Algernon you're in!"
    And the Deb's Delight
    Did India proud that night!

Rhythm continues softly

Mind you, Pater was a great moralist. His philosophy for life was never

Act I   3

take anything out without putting something back in... I like to think I've followed the code ... particularly with chorus girls... Never take one out without at least trying! (*He sings* Deb's Delight)
> She had some coconuts
> Set on a sawdust mark
> And so just for a lark
> I played her game.
>
> She said a tanner will buy
> Three balls with which to shy
> And I watched her bosom sigh
> In sheer delight.
>
> And I won a teddy bear
> Yet I had one ball to spare
> And the Deb's Delight knocked plenty off that night.
> Yes, the Deb's Delight knocked plenty off that ni-i-ight,
> Yes, the Deb's Delight knocked plenty off that night!

Troop takes a bow, then...

Black-out

Music Cue No 3

The Lights come up on the sitting-room of a private nursing home. There are a couple of odd armchairs, a settee, a footstool and a small table. An upright piano stands in the corner. A large window is UL. *A screen* UC. *A transportable payphone* DL. *This isn't the main residents' lounge but an under-used sitting-room*

> *Stephanie enters furtively* L. *She is in her mid-twenties and wears the dress-cum-uniform of a nursing home assistant*

She goes to the phone and lifts the receiver. She puts in a coin and dials, all the time listening for anyone approaching

Stephanie (*into the phone*) Yes, shit-face, it's me. Shut up and listen! Money, in a word. Not for me, for Andrew. You don't bring kids into this world to starve. ... I know, but I don't see why I should subsidise your adultery. Turns prostitution on its head that does. ... No, I didn't say she was a prostitute. Prostitutes have the decency to send 'em back when they've finished with 'em... Oh! And tell her not to wear white tights. ...

No, I haven't seen her but a friend of mine has. Looked like she was wearing cricket pads! (*She listens*)

Troop is heard singing softly behind the screen

Troop (*singing*) You'll see me often
    Out in high-class places
    At the races
    Or by the sea...

Shocked Stephanie freezes

Stephanie (*into the phone*) Got to go... Money and quick! Or I'll make a nuisance of myself. (*She hangs up and approaches the screen warily*)

She removes the screen carefully to reveal snoozing Troop. He wears a heavy dressing-gown and sits in a wheelchair, a walking stick on his lap

Oh, you're here, are you? Look at it! Death's rehearsal... Still, what else can he do but kip? (*She looks at sleeping Troop*) Is it cruel to make you live so long? (*She shakes Troop gently*) Hey! Wakey-wakey!
Troop (*rousing*) Wha'?
Stephanie I've to ask what you want for your dinner. And you missed bingo.
Troop Who are you? And who let you backstage ... Norman?

Stephanie tidies papers and magazines and will stack them on the table

Stephanie It's lamb ... with carrots and boiled potatoes. Or there's fish.
Troop I don't know you.
Stephanie Snap! Don't know you, either... I'm Stephanie. Been here a week. You've not noticed because you've slept the clock round.
Troop Have you seen Muddlecombe?
Stephanie Don't know a Muddlecombe. Is she staff?
Troop He's my cat.
Stephanie Could still be staff, the money they're paying! No, love, no Muddlecombe. We've Bagshaw, Burgess, Everson, Hindley, Jackman, Lawrence, Murdoch... When they finish the extension we'll take more in and I'll lose track. Till then, I'm *au fait* alphabetical.

Troop watches as Stephanie finishes tidying

Troop Norman usually brings me a Guinness. I'm on again in half an hour.

Stephanie crosses to the phone and lifts the receiver

Act I 5

Stephanie Don't let on about this, OK? Not allowed to use residents' facilities.
Troop They've promised sunshine. That'll bring 'em in. Where's this?
Stephanie Where's what?
Troop Here?
Stephanie Home. Where your heart is.
Troop If it's home, he should be here. (*He struggles to his feet, calling*) Muddlecombe! Muddlecombe!
Stephanie (*replacing the receiver*) Look, Mister ... er... Why don't you have your dinner first, eh?

Troop is poking about the furniture with his stick

Troop Muddlecombe! Muddlecombe! Where are you, you bugger?
Stephanie Hey!
Troop He's probably with her. Look out the window.
Stephanie What you talking about?
Troop I'm talking about straying... meandering. Putting it about like there's no bloody tomorrow. Should have him separated from his knackers. That'd teach him.

Stephanie's eyes roll heavenward

So look out the window. See if he's there.
Stephanie There's no cat, honest. Matron won't have cats.
Troop Go on, girl! I'm employing you!
Stephanie (*trying to steer Troop to the chair*) Give it a week, eh? More kip, more treatment and all this agitation'll be behind you. Be as catatonic as the rest, I promise.
Troop (*struggling free*) Gerroff!
Stephanie Oh! Spirited, are we? Have to increase your daily dose of happy pills.

She watches Troop slowly lower himself into the chair and lapse into silence

Matron's worried about you. You don't mingle, don't talk. Just shut yourself away in here and sleep.

No response from Troop

You have to eat, you know. Tell me what you want for your dinner and I'll look for your cat. Not with any great enthusiasm, but I'll go through the motions... How's that?

Troop If this is home then he should be here. Always here.
Stephanie When I said "home", I meant Havencrest Home. You know, for the elderly.

Troop doesn't respond. Stephanie is a bit at sea

   Tell you what, I'll put you down for the fish. It makes brains... Live in hope, eh, Mister ... er...

Pause. Stephanie goes to the window

   What's his name again? Your cat.
Troop Eh? Oh! Muddlecombe... Can you see him? Black and white Tom with scar tissue.

Stephanie goes through the motions of looking through the window

Stephanie No... No sign. Trees, trees, and more trees.
Troop House in the corner. Fancy lace and pink window-box. He's sniffing after the Siamese strumpet that lives there... Can you see it?
Stephanie No.
Troop Crane your neck.

Stephanie cranes her neck in exaggerated fashion

Stephanie I'm craning. No joy.
Troop (*struggling to his feet*) Can't miss it. Gardenfull of piss-potted geraniums.

Stephanie, aware that Troop's now closer, makes a more positive effort to look obliquely through the window, then humours him

Stephanie Oh, yes. Got it.
Troop See Muddlecombe?
Stephanie No.
Troop See the window-box?
Stephanie Yes. Lovely splash of colour.
Troop See the gnome?
Stephanie Who?
Troop The gnome in the window-box? Him fishing for fresh air with a weather cone.
Stephanie Oh, yes... Amazing what you can see when you put your mind to it.

Act I

Troop Bloody decadence!
Stephanie (*moving from the window*) The gnome?
Troop Muddlecombe! Rather be there than here.
Stephanie Does he ever catch anything?
Troop Eh?
Stephanie The gnome ... fishing?
Troop Ay, pneumonia every time the gutter leaks. If he's playing it for laughs he's dying on his arse! (*He shuffles to the window and peers out. Then he turns slowly, clearly confused*) Where am I?
Stephanie (*going close to Troop*) Don't worry. You're being well cared for.
Troop Who am I? Say it so I'll remember.
Stephanie (*returning Troop to the chair*) Sorry, love, I've only been here a week.
Troop (*feigning lightness*) Rum do, eh? Don't know who, don't know where.
Stephanie I do know you. If you know what I mean. I've seen you every day.
Troop (*sitting*) But can't place the face, eh? Could be who I like, I suppose.
Stephanie I'll find out. (*She takes in the room*) Never looks straight, this place. (*She busies herself tidying again*)
Troop Rhett Butler, Genghis Khan... I could be anyone.
Stephanie Told you. I'll find out. Give me time.
Troop How much time do you think I've got, eh? Attend the funeral and all you'll learn is who I used to be. Even then they might not have it right... I'm a discard, aren't I?
Stephanie You mustn't think like that. Being old might have its privileges but self-pity shouldn't be one of them. What are you—seventy? Seventy-five? Eighty?
Troop Twenty-nine!
Stephanie Well, you've had a damn sight longer than I've had, that's for sure. Think about it. I could fall under a bus tomorrow. The bomb could go off. Fate could rob me of my allotted time. You've beaten Fate, haven't you? Count your blessings.

Troop watches her tidying a moment

Troop Hired as some sort of cheerleader, are you?
Stephanie It's the natural order of things. People live, then they die. Some live long, some short. Life's a lottery and you drew a winning ticket... With me?
Troop Think I've got the gist, ay... You come in here every morning, take one look at me and curse to buggery the fact that you can stand up without falling over... Hard luck! Stay jealous!
Stephanie Each of us has to move over when our time comes... Is it OK if I put you down for the fish?

Troop No... wait... I'm anxious. Not about dying. Just dying anonymous... You're right. I had a life an' half. Can't grumble. Memories enough to fill a library if I could catch 'em... I had greatness in me... You've been sent, haven't you?
Stephanie Yes, Matron sent me to find out what you want for your dinner.
Troop (*struggling to his feet*) No, no... Greater powers sent you. Sent you to help me. Don't let 'em bury a lie... Look at me. Go on.

Stephanie looks at Troop

Stephanie So?
Troop Do you recognize me?
Stephanie 'Course I do. Seen you every day for a week. Bit difficult now you've got your eyes open, but...
Troop (*impatiently*) No, no, I don't mean here.
Stephanie Don't know what you mean.

She watches as Troop slumps sadly back into his chair

I'm sorry.
Troop Who am I?
Stephanie You're ... er ... well, you're you. Who else would you be?
Troop (*sharply*) Who?

Inspiration strikes Stephanie. She goes behind Troop and looks into the collar of his dressing-gown

(*Struggling*) Gerroff! What you...?
Stephanie (*breaking away*) Mr Burgess.
Troop Eh?
Stephanie It's sewn inside your collar... Burgess.

Troop gets thoughtful

Troop Burgess, ay... Harold Burgess. I knew him once. I killed him.
Stephanie (*laughing*) Killed him?
Troop Stone dead. He was holding me back, y'see? Had to go. (*He lapses into silence*)

Stephanie watches him

Stephanie You're on vitamins. They'll help you remember... Look, Mister ... er ... you were here when I came. Wrong, I know, but I took it for granted you'd always been here. Part of the furniture. I'm sorry.

Act I 9

Troop I was playing Ramsgate. It'd be Ramsgate, ay. Norman was Ramsgate.
Stephanie You sing in your sleep. Did you know?
Troop (*amused*) Do I? I'll sing when I'm dead. Once a pro always a pro... Oh, ay! I'll go up there with my band parts, tip the MD half-a-bar and that's me fixed for a couple of extra choruses. (*He sings*)
 You'll see me often
 Out in high-class places
 At the races
 Or by the sea...
Management might stipulate eight minutes, act as known, but with a wink here, back-hander there, you can always milk it. The longer you can stay out under that spotlight the longer your public remembers you... They all do it, y'know? And what's good for one's good for Harry Troop.

Pause

Stephanie Harry Troop?
Troop Eh?
Stephanie Who's Harry Troop?
Troop Me! Read your programme.
Stephanie But you're Mr Burgess. We've established that.
Troop And I've told you he's dead... Go away, girl. Leave me.
Stephanie It's your memory, love... Memory, you see, is like a big tape recorder. Imagine a spool of tape that starts recording immediately you're born...
Troop (*interrupting*) Go away!
Stephanie Listen and learn! As old as you are! ...Small at first, but getting bigger and bigger the longer we live and the more experiences we experience. Until ... well, until, in your case, it's very big.
Troop Where is it, this tape?
Stephanie In your head.
Troop Fuse must've gone. Can't remember a bloody thing.
Stephanie That's because you're old.
Troop Oh, I can remember that!
Stephanie (*sailing on*) ...and the tape's rewinding... What happened yesterday?

Troop can't recall

Or last week? Or last year? Don't know, do you? That's because your memory's been erased. Rewound beyond the point of recollection.
Troop Technical stuff, eh?

Stephanie And once it starts rewinding, it's almost impossible to get it back in the record mode.
Troop Cheerful that, isn't it?
Stephanie Want me to go on?
Troop Does it get any better?
Stephanie Not really. You won't remember anyway.
Troop Go on, then.
Stephanie So the memory tape rewinds to what it first recorded. Your childhood and your youth... My grandmother couldn't remember what she'd had for her tea but she could talk for hours about the time she worked in a laundry. Know how old she was when she did that?
Troop Had her tea?
Stephanie Worked in the laundry.
Troop I don't think I ever knew your grandmother.
Stephanie Seventeen... Could be, you know, that by the time we die, the tape's rewound ready for our next life... Reincarnation... Should cheer you up, that. You might come back as someone else.
Troop Come back? It's who I'm going as that bothers me.
Stephanie You're Burgess.
Troop Sod Burgess! OK, so God's an electrician, but that doesn't solve my earthly dilemma, does it? Here's home, you said. Not my home.
Stephanie It is. And your name's Harold Burgess. Sorry I can't be more informative, but I've got work to do. (*She goes towards exit* L)
Troop You don't care and the world's forgot... I was like you once. And I did things.

Stephanie stops and looks at Troop

I don't deserve to be dumped, ignored, deserted. (*He struggles to his feet*) Not self-pity, young woman. I just want my identity restored before it's too late.
Stephanie Look... Matron——
Troop (*interrupting firmly*) Sod bloody Matron! Singer's on his feet... Maybe on his arse, but sod bloody Matron! I speak for me. Remember that.

Pause as Stephanie and Troop confront each other. Stephanie relaxes

Stephanie Right... OK... So is it lamb or is it fish? I just want a decision.
Troop Oh ay? And how do you propose to get that? Force? Bribery? Seduction?

Stephanie can't resist laughing in spite of herself. Troop starts to laugh too

There y'are, see! Few more like you and I've got an epitaph... Help me.

Act I

Stephanie I'm busy.
Troop (*agitated*) While there's still time.
Stephanie (*placating*) All right ... all right... But you help me, OK? Make your mind up about your dinner.

Troop flops into the armchair

Troop Ay... The ramblings of just another old man, eh? Anathema to the ears of youth.

Stephanie watches as Troop dozes. She lights a cigarette. Surreptitiously, she goes to the phone. She lifts the receiver, puts in a coin and dials. She waits

Stephanie (*into the phone*) Hiya, Mandy. How is he? ... No, don't disturb him. Just give him a big love from his mum when he wakes up. Miss him like hell, but needs must... Called shit-face earlier about the maintenance. ... God no, I didn't tell him about the job. Might not stick it anyway, it's so bloody awful. ... Not me at all, kid, no... More like a chapel of rest than a nursing home. ... Matron's a bit of a tartar. Keeps yawning on about progressive geriatric care.... What? ... Well, that means bingo, doesn't it? Sing-alongs, the odd entertainer. Don't know why they don't build them an assault course... A scream on the veranda yesterday. (*Amused*) No, listen. Had the poor old souls playing comb and paper... God! Went down like dominoes the lot of 'em... Don't know whether they were really asleep or just shamming... Well, I might sham myself if some silly bugger had me playing comb and paper at that age! ... No, Matron seemed quite happy. "Wouldn't get that on the National Health", she said. "Not these days." Silly cow! ... Money's going. See you, Mandy. Kiss Andrew for me. ... Bye. (*She hangs up and contemplates the snoozing Troop*) Anyway, Mister Whatever-your-name-is... Perhaps you'll make your mind up and let me know what you want ... eventually.

Stephanie exits L

Troop (*rousing drowsily*) What I want? Eh? (*Loudly*) What I want? Tell you what I don't want. I don't want to be here.

Music Cue No 4. *Rattle of tambourine offstage. Troop reacts*

Mam? (*Cri de coeur*) No use, Mam! My bag's packed and my mind's made up. I'll not die a nobody!

The Lights darken slightly. Tambourine rattles again off

Music Cue No 5. *Salvation Army music is heard. Troop rises shakily*

(*Confused*) Understand. I want you to understand. Break the mould, I've got to... You've got your faith, your calling. Well, I'm being called, Mam ... ay ... called, shouted ... urged to quit this poet's excuse for bloody Jerusalem and let some light into my life. Be ambitious for me!

Music Cue No 6. *Salvation Army music fades. Tambourine gives a prolonged rattle off, receding*

(*Calling*) Mam? I'm not Burgess. Not anymore. I left him with the cobbles, the poverty, the factory dirt sticking to wet donkeystone... Not Burgess! Reborn—Harry Troop, alias Algernon Beckwith-Smythe, the Deb's Delight. (*He listens. Quieter*) Mam? (*He sings softly*)
    You'll see me often
    Out in high-class places
    At the races
    Or by ... the sea... (*His song peters out*)

Troop moves back towards the chair as Stephanie enters L. *She carries a mug of tea in one hand and a duster and polish in the other*

Stephanie Hey! I've been catching up. Just glimpsed your notes.

Unresponsive Troop moves past her

  Born in Todmorden. Right?
Troop No.

Stephanie puts the tea on the table near his chair

Stephanie I've read it, Mr Burgess.
Troop Name's Harry Troop. Born at the end of some long-demolished pier... Did you hear the Salvationist?
Stephanie Who?
Troop My mam? With her tambourine?

Stephanie gives him a long look

Oh, she was here all right! On a mission. And the Lord sayeth that no conscience shall go unmolested, no guilt unridden... Ay... Give her one grain of regret and Mam's in there to reap a bloody harvest... Told me to go, you know. Booted me out... Be independent, she said. Make a name for yourself.

Act I   13

Stephanie Go out into the world and multiply—as the maths teacher said to the rabbit. (*She laughs, moving to the piano to polish it*)

Po-faced Troop looks at her... She looks at him and her laughter dries up

   Thought you liked a good laugh.
Troop First rule of comedy. Leave the laughter to your audience.
Stephanie Sorry. Couldn't resist it.
Troop Second rule. Resist the irresistible.
Stephanie Oh? Expert on jokes now, are we?
Troop It was my job.
Stephanie (*disbelieving*) Gerroff!

Pause as Troop stares belligerently at Stephanie

Troop Why did the rabbit laugh?
Stephanie Don't know. Why did the rabbit laugh?
Troop Because it had a hare up its arse!

Stephanie finds this hilarious... Po-faced Troop stares at her, then flops into the chair

Stephanie Hey! You're good.
Troop Keep laughing. It might help me remember... Mam knew me as Harold, y'know?
Stephanie As good a name as any.
Troop But that's what they'll call me when I get up there. (*He points heavenward with his stick*) Harold Burgess. There's nowt down for Harold Burgess. He's a blank page. A man should be judged on what he achieved. I was Harry Troop, for Godsake! I topped the bill.
Stephanie Being new, I didn't think Matron would let me see. The notes, I mean. They're confidential.
Troop But it's not me. Don't you see? They've sewn a bloody alias into my dressing gown.

Pause

Stephanie And you're not on your own. You've a daughter. Edith.
Troop Edith, ay. (*He taps his temple*) Lives up here.
Stephanie She lives down South.
Troop Suppose she put me in this place.
Stephanie Look, love, I don't know the details. Whatever happened it was for your own good. Your daughter's all you've got. I've just read it.

Troop You'll get no truth from Edith. Not about me, you won't. Preaches the gospel according to filial alienation, does Edith. Dumps me in here under an assumed dressing gown and pisses off back to Staines.
Stephanie I can't discuss it. Told you, it's confidential.
Troop Listen to me... I want you to use your imagination and put yourself in my position. I'm soon to face my Maker. Bearing in mind His influence, He'll get advanced warning of my coming... Are you with me?
Stephanie Ahead of you, I think... When you get up there you want your name in lights at God's music hall... I'm your nurse, love, not your manager.

Troop sits back, amused at this. Stephanie starts stripping covers off scatter cushions

Troop Are you wed?
Stephanie Not really.
Troop Marry me and you'll want for nothing.
Stephanie No thanks. Tried it. He ran off with a canteen manageress.
Troop Ran off, ay. Even memories run off when they tire of talking to you.
Stephanie He keeps asking to see Andrew but why should I let him?
Troop And when memory fails, you fall back on fantasy. How it was. How you'd have liked it to be.
Stephanie Visits to the zoo. Wet Sundays in McDonald's. Not putting Andrew through all that.
Troop Edith puts me through it. Depends who they believe.
Stephanie And who would we be doing it for, eh? Not Andrew. Certainly not me... No... Dads only remain dads while they're under the same roof as their offspring.
Troop Told her not to marry him, didn't I? Begged her.
Stephanie Sorry?
Troop Saw through him, y'see. First day I met him, I saw straight through him.
Stephanie Does she ever visit? Edith?
Troop Not visit as such. Edith's more for visitation... Is she still with the rubber planter?
Stephanie Who's the rubber planter?
Troop Fella she married.
Stephanie I don't know.
Troop Asked Edith once what he did for a living. "He's something in property", she said. Edith all over. Got a knack for indirect speech... "What in property?" I said. "A damp course? Sash-cord window?"

Stephanie is amused. Pause as Troop goes quiet. Stephanie watches him

Act I

Never thought I'd end up like this... If they could see me now, eh? All them holiday-makers in deck-chairs. Laughing, clapping, sun always shining. The world stood still on its axis just waiting for that curtain to go up... Overture and beginners, please! You always got butterflies... Oh, ay... Three shows a day but don't let any of 'em kid you they're not nervous... Ask your mother, she'll tell you.
Stephanie (*puzzled*) Mr Troop...

Music Cue No 6A

Troop (*reacting off* R) I'm coming! (*He rises gingerly to his feet. To Stephanie*) Catch the act then I'll take you on the rifles. Win you a rag doll.
Stephanie (*uncertainly*) Please... Mr Burgess...

Troop goes to exit R, *then checks himself. He gets agitated*

Troop The stage... Which way? They're playing my music... Help me!

Music Cue No 7. *"Grey" Edith saunters on* L, *unseen. She is cold, distant, contemptuous. She moves slowly, insidiously, testing the furniture for dust like some sadistic sergeant-major. She is a figment of Troop's conscience, invisible to Stephanie*

Get your mother!
Edith Mum's dead. You know that, Dad.

Troop freezes. Edith watches, smiling, as Stephanie gently takes hold of the agitated Troop

Stephanie C'mon, love... It's OK. (*She steers him back to the chair*)
Troop The punters. They're waiting.
Stephanie (*comforting*) Just relax. I'm here.
Troop (*now seated*) Edith?
Edith Here as summoned, Dad.
Stephanie Now don't move. I'll not be a sec'. (*She tries to go*)

Troop grabs her hand

Troop (*emotionally*) You're stitching me up... Sending me up there under false pretences.
Stephanie (*out of her depth, putting her arm round him*) God'll know. He knows everything.
Troop I topped the bill.
Stephanie He'll know that too... Just sit still. I'll get Matron.

Troop I don't want strangers!
Edith That's all you can rely on, Dad. Them that know you won't be in a hurry to buy tickets.
Troop They only know what they've been told. You're no daughter of mine. Poisoned the well, you have.
Edith Queuing three deep in heaven. All waiting for the great Harry Troop... Good reviews, do you think?

Stephanie tucks the blanket round Troop's legs

Stephanie Maybe Matron'll let you have the phone ... ring your daughter.
Troop Daughter! There's a joke! (*To Edith*) Takes you all your time to remember my birthday. Five pairs of slippers in that wardrobe. Five pairs, all brand new! I'm your father, damn you, not a bloody caterpillar! Go on, sod off!

Confused, Stephanie hands a newspaper to Troop

Stephanie Here... It's today's.

He puts himself tetchily behind the paper and feigns reading

Mr Burgess?
Troop Shut it!
Stephanie Mr Troop... I'm Stephanie. I work here, remember? I'm sure your daughter keeps in touch. I'll check, if you like.
Edith Dotage. And still hungry for celebrity.
Troop (*behind the paper*) No crime in wanting the record straight.
Edith But there's danger. If you remember, they all remember. That what you want?
Troop (*to Stephanie*) Don't listen to her.
Stephanie (*confused*) Who?

Troop lowers the paper

Troop (*to Stephanie*) Says here... Listen! Ignore her... Says here. (*He reads*) "Claustrophobic man beats up wife". Probably try that in open court. (*He anxiously glances at Edith then hides back behind the paper*)

Amused, Stephanie gets closer to Troop. She gently lowers the paper

(*Tetchily*) Eh!

Edith wanders over to the piano as Stephanie speaks

Act I   17

Stephanie You're a very funny man.
Troop (*confidentially to Stephanie*) I topped the bill. (*He glances suspiciously towards Edith*)
Stephanie I know… You're also reading the paper upside down.

She adjusts the paper for Troop who keeps a wary eye on Edith

Troop Ah, yes, thank you, very much. Then today'll be Wednesday…
Stephanie It's Friday.
Troop Same difference. Monday and Tuesday, y'see, I read it sideways. Sat'day I do alternate lines. Sunday I put it to music and sing it down the plug-hole.

Stephanie laughs and moves away

Stephanie OK now?
Troop Don't worry. I'm impervious to iconoclasts.
Stephanie Good.

Stephanie exits L

Music Cue No 8. *Echoing piano, off, plays* Waltz Around the Floor. *Troop reacts*

Troop Don't play that! Don't ever play that!
Edith (*amused*) You wrote it. Or stole it. Anyway, I thought you wanted to be remembered.

Troop gets shakily to his feet, shuffles agitatedly to the piano. He strikes the closed piano lid with his stick. Music ends abruptly. Edith moves away, laughing

Troop There's stronger voices than yours. Fairer judges. Played no part in my life, now you want to hijack my death… I'm not listening.

Female laughter is heard echoing offstage, behind Troop. He reacts

That your mother? (*Tense, he listens*)

Silence

Edith No… This one didn't need band parts. Good enough to just busk it along… Remember?

Troop (*calling*) Jessie?
Edith It's Stella. Dear, darling Stella... I did warn you. If you remember, they all remember.

Laughter echoes off again

Is she laughing with or laughing at, do you think?

Laughter fades... Troop keeps a wary eye on Edith as she moves behind him

Difficult to tell, isn't it? Particularly for one who fed so much of himself to unreality.
Troop Blessed is the comedian for he shall know the joy of never being taken seriously.
Edith Until now.
Troop They loved me. Came back again and again.
Edith And paid well for the privilege. Others paid too, didn't they?
Troop I'm paying now. You've got me here under Burgess.
Edith Why not? My father was Harold Burgess. It's official. Indelible. Says so on my birth certificate... Don't provoke the spirits, Dad. Take refuge in Burgess.
Troop But I'm not Burgess. Nobody's heard of bloody Burgess!
Edith A blessing, believe me.
Troop Harry Troop made laughter, gave pleasure.
Edith Harry Troop was an illusion. Those backstage knew you for what you were.

Sad, Troop flops into the chair

Troop Leave me. I want to die in peace.
Edith Harry Troop can't do that. Too many memories. But nobody ever takes a comedian seriously, do they? Let's remember together.
Troop No!
Edith A light-hearted reminiscence from that doyen of the variety stage, Harry Troop.
Troop Don't mock.
Edith Tall tales of theatrical digs and harridan landladies...
Troop ...it fed and clothed you.
Edith Chilly Sundays on Crewe Station...
Troop All o' that, yes.
Edith A fraternity without envy...
Troop Yes...
Edith ...enveloped in the warm affection of an adoring public.

Act I 19

Troop I worked for that…
Edith Music, laughter and the opium of applause…
Troop Three tiers of indifference that only became an audience when I made 'em listen…
Edith …and never an argument about billing.
Troop No!

Edith laughs. Troop stares at her

I never argued about billing?
Edith Didn't you?
Troop In the early days I was too humble. And when I was known it wasn't necessary. Never a need to argue about billing.
Edith There's one that might dispute that. She's there, Dad. Hovering in the wings of eternity. (*She goes towards the exit* R)
Troop You can't leave it like this. (*He struggles to his feet*) Listen to me!
Edith How it was? Or how you'd have liked it to be?

Amused, Edith exits R

Her laughter echoes after her

Troop (*calling after Edith*) Prefer rumour to the word of your own father, d'you? Nice girl was Stella Turner, clever with it. No acrimony.

Stella's laughter begins echoing behind Troop, mingling for a moment with Edith's. Confused and anxious Troop reacts to this. Then Edith's laughter fades, leaving only Stella's. He reacts to this change of tone and direction. Pause, as Troop listens

(*Calling*) Edith? Edith? Stella?

Music Cue No 9

The laughter fades. Troop listens

(*To the silence, quietly*) Stella…

Soulmates *is played low and slow. Confused, Troop tries to find direction, then moves towards exit* R

(*Over the music*) Don't go, Stella… I'm begging you. Don't go!

Stella, offstage, sings the echoing second verse of Soulmates—*slow tempo*

Stella (*off; singing*) Soulmates, walking through life we are
        Soulmates, following friendship's star
        Call mates, to see us any time at all...

Singing offstage fades as the Light reduces. Troop stands a moment, confused

Troop (*going towards exit* R) Stella? Wait... Stella! They've got me here under Burgess.

Troop exits R

Black-out

Soulmates *played low and slow as the Light grows bright. The set has taken on the semblance of a dressing-room. The mirror becomes a dressing mirror, surrounded by bulbs*

Troop enters L. *He's young, energetic and wears a natty blazer. He carries a stick and straw hat and will put on a clip dickie-bow at the mirror*

The music fades

What's your game, eh? Bluff? Think you can walk in here and burgle my self-respect? I'll lay my cards against yours any day of the week and chance it. So you can sod off now and take your anonymity with you...

Stella emerges from behind the screen. She wears tap shoes, short skirt and is buttoning up her blouse top. She will push Troop away from the mirror and check her make-up—ensuing exchanges take place as they prepare to go on stage

    I've never heard of Stella Turner.
Stella Snap! I've never heard of Harry Troop.
Troop There's plenty that have.
Stella It's them that sent me. Not my idea we should form a double. They say God makes 'em and pairs 'em. Not in this business. Your soddin' agent does it.
Troop My agent said we should give it a try.
Stella Correction... He said he wouldn't get you another booking till you'd found yourself a partner... Three years touring a solo and still sharing bottom with the printer... My God! If anyone needs help, you do, love. I'm your salvation ... I've got style, sophistication, and can time a line.

Act I   21

Troop Just time your next tram and piss off!
Stella You've proved you can't make it on your own. You need me.
Troop I'm grateful.
Stella Face it, Troopie, you're a soddin' no-hoper. *Deb's Delight* and all that crap went out with George Leybourne. It's about change, novelty... I'll give you six months.
Troop Make it life and promise not to visit.
Stella Stick with me and you might play south of Burnley.
Troop You'll never make it with your modesty.
Stella I'm in a hurry.
Troop Watch you don't meet yourself coming back!
Stella Met you, haven't I? Where've you been that didn't pay you off on the Tuesday?

Each contemplates the other a moment

Well? When do we start?
Troop Now. (*He glances at his watch*) We'll have a minute's silence in memory of your tact and diplomacy!
Stella Turner and Troop.
Troop Harry Troop and Stella.
Stella Is that your last word?
Troop No, I'm saving that. It's a beauty!
Stella Six months, then we'll think again.

Black-out

Music Cue No 10

A spot snaps on DS. *Pit music is* Soulmates *played up-tempo. Twinkling showtime lights along footlights and around proscenium. Troop moves into the spot, beaming out at the audience*

Troop (*announcing above the music*) Ladies and gentlemen. Troop's the name, laughter's the game! Will you please give a very special welcome to my dear, darling partner, Miss Stella Turner!

Music Cue No 11

A spot snaps on Stella, upstage from Troop. She comes down to join him and they go into a quick-fire patter act

Stella Well, Harry, long time no see, eh? As the kipper said to the fishmonger. Been avoiding me, have you?

Troop Nonsense, Stella. How's your mother?
Stella Still got her cold.
Troop Should put Vic on her chest.
Stella Can never find him. Always out gambling.
Troop Oh, dear. Plays the gee-gees, does he?
Stella No, the accordion.
Troop The accordion?
Stella Outside the pub. Bets punters they can't name a tune he can't play.
Troop I suppose he knows that's illegal.
Stella Know it? He can play all three verses.
Troop Tell me more about your mother.
Stella She won't go to Dr Drake.
Troop Why won't she go to Dr Drake?
Stella She says he's a quack. Dr Clune's a lune and Dr Kirk's a berk.
Troop I was going to ask about Dr Pratt but I don't think I'll bother... Your mother definitely needs treatment.
Stella Well you know she's a kleptomaniac.
Troop Oh dear! What's she taking for it?
Stella Anything that isn't nailed down.
Troop Where are you and your mother living now?
Stella Clay Street. We've got the first floor.
Troop The first floor? Who lives underneath?
Stella The man with the allergies.
Troop And what's he allergic to?
Stephanie Landlords, bailiffs, tallymen.
Troop Does he come out in a rash?
Stella Think so. Mum's always saying, "Hallo! He's been spotted".
Troop See much of your dad?
Stella Oh no. Mum's had him arrested.
Troop Arrested? What for?
Stella Well, she never liked him.
Troop No.
Stella But the copper would never have caught him if he'd been wearing his own trousers.
Troop Really? So the policeman had someone else's trousers on?
Stella No, my father. It was Sybil's fault.
Troop Sybil?
Stella She had one of her brainstorms and threw the chamber downstairs.
Troop Nasty.
Stella Anyway, she said he wasn't coming back and slammed the door.
Troop Hold on, hold on... Who's Sybil?
Stella My mother calls her my father's washer.
Troop Don't you mean scrubber?

Act I   23

Stella No, washer. Because she's always on the tap.
Troop Go on.
Stella So after the chamber had gone...
Troop (*interrupting*) Just a minute, just a minute... Who's the chamber?
Stella Sybil's lodger. They call him the chamber, you see...
Troop ⎫
         ⎬ (*together*) ...because everyone thinks he's potty!
Stella ⎭
Troop (*to the audience*) You get the hang of it after a bit.
Stella I'm not keeping you, am I?
Troop No, no. Train's not till ten.
Stella You catching a train?
Troop Throwing myself under it! You were saying?
Stella About my father's trousers.
Troop Of course.
Stella My father had them on when the copper mistook him for someone else.
Troop He thought he was Sybil's lodger.
Stella Who?
Troop The policeman.
Stella Oh, no. I don't think the policeman ever lodged with Sybil.
Troop I meant your father.
Stella But my father doesn't take lodgers.
Troop (*to the audience*) My horoscope said I shouldn't bother waking up this morning.
Stella No... The policeman, you see, thought my father was the lodger.
Troop Did he?
Stella He was wanted for illegal entry.
Troop Entering the trousers without permission.
Stella Breaking into the fairground.
Troop Into the fairground? What made him do that?
Stella Thinks he's a big wheel.
Troop I see.
Stella In a roundabout sort of way.
Troop Of course. Did they catch him?
Stella Oh, yes. They grabbed him by the dodgems.
Troop Saves using the handcuffs, I suppose.
Stella But he escaped and ran into the marquee.
Troop Then what did he do?
Stella Nothing. He just hung around in there till the coppers came.
Troop So he dashed into the marquee and just hung around... What did they charge him with?
Stella Loitering with intent.
Troop Sing the song, Stella.

Music Cue No 12

Troop and Stella sing Soulmates

Troop and Stella (*singing*) Soulmates, walking through life we are
                            Soulmates, following friendship's star
                            Call mates, to see us anytime at all.

   Because we're Soulmates,
   Go along hand in hand
   Soulmates, come along join the band
   Make dates, and bring the family too

   And whether you're stalls or gallery
   You will always see
   Harry and Stella in perfect harmony
   Soulmates true!

Troop and Stella dance then reprise the last verse

   And whether you're stalls or gallery
   You will always see
   Harry and Stella in perfect harmony
   Soulmates true!

Troop and Stella take bows and music plays them off R

Black-out

Soulmates *is played softly, reduced in tempo. The Lights come up on the sitting-room*

Music Cue No 12B

Real Edith sits on the settee, reading a magazine. A shopping bag is at her feet

Old Troop shuffles on R. *He wears a dressing-gown and carries his stick*

Edith discards the magazine and rises

Edith Hallo, Dad.

Troop starts. Then he stares hard at Edith

   Well? Don't I get a kiss?

Act I

Agitated, Troop moves past her, and sits in his chair

Troop Still twisting the knife, are you? Oh, there may have been acrimony to begin with, but after that me and Stella got on like house on fire. Professional, you understand. Always professional. And when she left for pastures new, she went with my blessing.
Edith (*with her shopping bag*) I've not come to argue, Dad. Even if I did know what you're talking about... I've brought you some fruit. And some detective books.
Troop What about the chest expanders?
Edith (*amused*) Don't be silly.
Troop Spent a career being silly.
Edith The boys would've come with me but Toby's just started in a solicitor's office and Ben's got exams. They send their love.
Troop He with you?
Edith Who?
Troop The rubber planter?
Edith Derek's not a rubber planter, Dad. You know that. And the dislike isn't mutual.
Troop Since when did I read detective books? When?
Edith Try. It'll help you concentrate.
Troop I see... Whodunits for the man who did it. Clever that.
Edith How've you been keeping? Matron tells me——
Troop (*interrupting*) Don't flannel me, Edith. Look around. Just you and me. No need for flannel. Haunt me. Go on. Tell me I'm a murderer.
Edith Oh, and something else. (*She roots in her bag and extracts a scrapbook*) Your scrapbook. (*She hands the book to Troop*)

He contemplates her

Not my idea. They think it might help.
Troop What's your game, then?
Edith Look, Dad. I've changed trains three times and left my umbrella in a taxi. No game, believe me.
Troop First you're against, then you're all for. Not one to change your mind without motive... So, c'mon... What is it?
Edith It's a good idea, that's what it is. Are you saying I should take it back? (*She reaches for the book*)
Troop (*hugging the book*) No! Proof positive this is. They can't deny me now. Not unless you stick the boot in... It's your angle that's confusing me. Blows your conspiracy.
Edith There's no conspiracy.
Troop (*pointedly*) Hiding me away under a pseudonym.

Stephanie enters L *as Troop thumbs through the book*

Stephanie Oh, so you found him then?
Edith My lucky day. Matron tells me you two have struck up quite a friendship.
Stephanie He makes me laugh.
Edith He has his moments... Seems I've had another wasted journey. He's in one of his moods.
Troop (*to Stephanie*) Come here. Look at this. (*He shows her the book*) The life and times of Harry Troop.
Stephanie (*to Edith*) Great! You brought it, then?
Edith Matron's wish is my command.
Troop Matron? What's it to do with Matron?
Edith Last time I rang she asked if I had any old photographs. I said you'd once compiled a scrapbook and she asked if I'd bring it.
Troop (*to Stephanie*) Do you know about this?
Stephanie 'Course I do. Part of Matron's rehabilitation programme.
Troop Rehabilitation? For what?
Stephanie We look at the pictures together, staff and residents. Then we talk about old times. Well, your old times, anyway. Helps you remember and gives us insight into what you got up to in your younger days.
Edith I told him it was a good idea.
Troop Rehabilitation, my arse!
Edith Dad!
Troop I don't need a refresher course in old age! Tell Matron I'm gawping at no-one else's pictures. This book'll speak for me. But I'll only to speak to them I choose to speak to.
Stephanie (*amused*) Don't get coy, Mr Burgess.

Troop gets tetchily to his feet

Edith (*aside*) Oh God!
Troop (*to Stephanie*) Thought so... She's got at you, hasn't she? Told you about this one. Been playing the dutiful daughter that long you can't see the performance. You were my last chance. Now she's nobbled you.
Stephanie (*to Edith*) What does he mean?
Edith It's a long story.
Troop Burgess! He's the fella in your files. (*He waves the book*) This is me! Harry Troop! When I face my Maker I'll appear according to my bill matter. Act as known. (*He clutches the book tightly to him*)

Stephanie guides him back into his chair. Troop sits tensely, hugging the book to his chest. Then he relaxes slightly, puts on his spectacles, and turns the pages. Stephanie and Edith move away

Act I   27

Stephanie He was telling me about his life on the stage. About him being a comedian... Mind if I ask you something?
Edith Go on.
Stephanie I'm new here and I'm not sure it's any of my business but... (*She hesitates*)
Edith Why is he so cantankerous and so antagonistic towards me?

Stephanie is silent

He lived with us briefly. In Staines, just after he gave up the bungalow. It was the first time we'd ever come in close contact... Family life was non-existent when I was a kid. Nature of his chosen profession... Anyway, it didn't work out. Easy to blame him, I suppose. He was old, set in his ways, a stranger almost.
Stephanie He is difficult sometimes.
Edith Half mad and wandering the district looking for a cat that died years ago... Have you got a family, Stephanie?
Stephanie Little boy. Andrew.
Edith Is he happy?
Stephanie Great, yeah, I think. He's four.
Edith Mine are in their teens. I had to choose... Does that make sense?
Stephanie Yeah... Natural, I suppose. Him resenting being put in here.
Edith He resents more than that... I'm all he has left. The last target. And he knows that my memories will outlive his. That's unbearable to him.
Stephanie Yeah ... well... I'll leave you to talk.
Edith Thanks, Stephanie.

Stephanie exits L

Edith walks back towards Troop

Troop (*enthused*) Hey! Come here... Picture of the Great Krakatoa. Dedicated to me personally. (*He reads*) "Best wishes to my good friend Harry Troop—Clacton 1934." Signed, "The Great Krakatoa"... He was a fire-eater and sword swallower. (*He turns the page*)

Edith watches him

Hey! And look at this. Done up as the Deb's Delight... Now that was taken at ... er...
Edith Margate, Dad.
Troop (*impatiently*) I know, I know. (*He turns the page*) There she is! Apart from your mother, she was the best partner I ever had... Stella Turner. (*He reminisces*) Y'know, me and Stella had something money can't buy.

Edith Rapport.
Troop How d'you know?
Edith Heard you say it so often.
Troop You're not right about me and Stella, y'know.
Edith I didn't know Stella, Dad.
Troop What's contained in that libellous mind of yours is contrary to the facts. Amicable. The parting was amicable. No acrimony.

Stella's laughter echoes offstage. Troop slams the book shut. He tenses up

Edith (*attempting diversion*) Dad? Show me that fire-eater again.
Troop You've brought her, haven't you?

Edith gently takes the book from Troop. He doesn't seem to notice

Edith What page was it? Hey, I could wear some of these dresses myself. Fashion doesn't change, does it? It just gets re-invented.
Troop (*loudly*) Don't blame me! Your own pigheadedness brought on your downfall, girl!

Edith puts the book down. She kneels by Troop

Stella, in dressing-gown, emerges from behind the screen, wiping her face with a towel

Edith Nobody's blaming you, Dad. How can I make you understand?
Stella Thought comics liked to be laughed at.
Troop I asked you to stay. Begged you!
Edith Whatever happened, happened a long time ago.
Troop Amicable. Amicable. I'm not listening.
Edith And I'm not staying if you're going to start this again… I'm sorry, Dad.
Stella Still a comic, aren't you, Harry? Or would you rather be my spirit guide and father confessor?

Amused, Stella goes back behind the screen

Troop (*holding on to Edith*) She was unmanageable. Managed her on stage. Worked, controlled, paced…
Edith (*comforting*) I know … shhhh…
Stella (*echoing off*) I've got style, sophistication and can time a line.
Troop (*loudly, agitated*) Couldn't time a bloody egg!
Edith Please, Dad. I've been travelling all day. Don't spoil it.

Act I   29

Troop It was my function, y'see...
Edith (*firmer*) Stop it, Dad!
Troop My function...
Edith (*rising*) I didn't come all this way for a re-run of your regrets. Change the subject or I go straight back to Staines... And that damn book goes with me!

Troop gets gingerly to his feet

Troop I was the power supply. We can all see the lamp burn, but who sees the electricity, eh? I was a word juggler, a verbal acrobat, Svengali with a funny walk... The feed!
Edith (*picking up the book*) Oh, for Godsake!
Troop Leave it!

Edith goes to defy him. Then he threatens her with the stick

I said, leave it... You're destroying me and I've a right to self-defence. If you love somebody, you forgive. But you don't love, d'you, Edith?
Edith You want more than love, Dad. You want something I can't give... Absolution.

Edith exits quickly L

Troop picks up the book. He goes back C, *thumbing through the book before pausing at one particular page*

Troop (*near tears*) You were a victim of your own impatience. You'd still have gone to America regardless of what I said... We were soulmates.
Stella (*echoing off*) What's soul, Harry? Have I got one?
Troop Soul? I don't know what it is, where it is. Perhaps talent and soul are the same thing. Knowing where to stand, when to speak. How best to catch the light.

The Light begins brightening and the sitting-room will take on the semblance of the dressing-room again. The window becomes the dressing-room mirror with lighted bulb surround. Troop closes the book and slowly begins taking off his dressing-gown

But one thing I do know. You need more than a fine bone structure, girl! (*He begins removing make-up at the mirror*)

Stella emerges from behind the screen in a black wraparound skirt and white blouse. She carries a suitcase which she puts in the dressing-room area. Then she barges Troop out of the way and applies lipstick at the mirror

Stella I've got more than that, Troopie old pal. I've got a better offer.
Troop You've also got a contract to adhere to.
Stella They'll buy me out of that.
Troop Not if I don't agree.
Stella It's as good as arranged.
Troop Not if I don't agree.
Stella You've no choice.
Troop Watch me! You signed, I signed. (*He gets the contract from the dressing-table drawer and reads*) "Conditions herein contained to be binding on all parties. Any additions, deletions or alternative conditions to be approved only after full discussion and mutual agreement."
Stella You bastard!
Troop (*reading on*) "No party to enter into any separate arrangement that could prove detrimental, either intentional or otherwise, to the terms and conditions outlined above."
Stella You're standing in my way.

Troop chucks the contract back in the drawer and slams it shut

Troop You think this flash Yank's after your talent? He'll need a bloody microscope to find it! He's a fake! A dream-monger! This business is crawling with 'em!
Stella What business? My God! You compare making films with what you're doing? Sorry, Troopie, I've got to tell you...
Troop (*interrupting*) Tell me what?
Stella You're at the arse-end, love! If you got paid by the laugh you'd be in the workhouse!
Troop There were laughs out there tonight. Plenty.
Stella But it's me they're laughing at.
Troop You're a puppet. Without my hand up your drawers you're less than nothing!
Stella (*stung*) You're being unfair, Harry.

Troop laughs derisively

(*Narked*) Never missed a call, never missed a cue, and always turned myself out decent... I've gone out there with my insides screaming.
Troop Your outside's not doing so bad.
Stella (*irately*) Boredom, frustration. Monday nights when the soddin' band outnumbered the audience. Friday nights when half of 'em were too pissed to listen... I've had it, Troopie! Had it!

Act I   31

Pause as Troop watches Stella lapse into breathless silence

Troop I'm asking you to stay. For your own sake... If this Yank's so interested he'll wait till we've played out the dates.
Stella I've told you. I'm in a hurry.
Troop And I've told you he's a fake.
Stella Know what your trouble is? You're possessive. Think you're my bloody keeper. Jealous of every bloke I ever took a fancy to. Treat me like a bloody nun.
Troop Thank you, Sister Hysteria!

Pause as Stella considers another tack

Stella Y'know, Harry, I've often wondered why you never tried your hand. I'm a very desirable property.
Troop Save it for the Yank.
Stella You should see some of the horny letters I get from punters.
Troop I'll read your memoirs.
Stella We've shared most things. Trains, digs, dressing-rooms. Never a hint as to what your feelings might be... What was it, Harry ... fear I might say "no"?

Troop lights a cigarette. Stella watches him

Troop Only one thing fears me, Stella.
Stella What's that, Harry?
Troop The truth. Telling you how I really feel about you going.
Stella Know what you mean. Being honest isn't something we artistes ever acquire a knack for, is it? But it's true about Morganheimer... Honest.
Troop Yeah.

Pause

Stella Tell me, Harry. About how you feel.
Troop And change the habit of a lifetime? We're in show business, Stella. Truth's a heresy.
Stella We're mates, Harry. Soulmates, supposed to be.
Troop Now you're getting sentimental.
Stella Never seen you like this. Could almost believe you like me.
Troop Respect you, Stella. You're good.
Stella Blimey! Praise from Harry Troop... Don't know what to say.
Troop Say "no" to the Yank.
Stella Forget Morganheimer. This is Harry Troop and Stella... Right, Harry?

Troop If I lost an arm or a leg I might still do it. Lose my timing, my voice, even my nerve, I'd take a holiday and hope. But losing you ... that's something that ... well... (*He breaks off*)
Stella Good team, eh?
Troop The best.
Stella How do we do it? What's the magic?
Troop Only idiots try to analyse comedy, Stella. You take it apart to find it and you end up with lots of bits you can't fit back together... Like soul, it's intangible.
Stella Funny, that's what he said.
Troop Who said?
Stella Morganheimer. About me.
Troop I thought we'd forgotten...
Stella (*sailing on*) Indefinable quality, he said. Don't ever question your talent, just trust it.
Troop I've told you, Stella——
Stella (*interrupting*) He wants to make me a star, Harry. Imagine that? Stella Turner in Hollywood?
Troop He's not interested in you, Stella. You're a plaything, a bit on the side.
Stella (*laughing*) They say confession's good for the soul, Harry. Feel better now?
Troop Go to hell!
Stella Hollywood, actually. I'll send you a postcard... Offer still holds good, Harry. Can still have me in lieu of contract.

Troop flops into the chair

Troop Keep it.
Stella Sort of going-away present.
Troop More notice I'd have got you something. Pair of collapsible knickers for your handbag!

Pause as Stella watches the silent Troop

Stella I'll settle for a favour.
Troop Don't wet yourself, I'll not press charges.
Stella Sweet of you, Harry. I really mean that, honest... Bit awkward, especially after all the nice things you've said.
Troop (*laughing*) Don't quote me, Stella. I was lying in my teeth. Nature of the business.
Stella Come off it!
Troop (*amused*) C'mon, Stella, it was a try-on. See how serious you were. You and me are finished anyway. A blind man with his head in a bag can see that.

Act I 33

Stella Finished?
Troop Tired, wrung-out.
Stella Crap!
Troop You wouldn't know, would you? Too busy counting laughs to gauge atmosphere... The act's lost its pace, Stella. I know because it's my job to know. It's become forced, predictable. Comedy's got to be fresh and ours has been on the slab too long.
Stella Then it's your fault.
Troop Probably.
Stella Not feeding me quick enough.
Troop Maybe.

Pause

Stella You're kidding again.
Troop Why kid? It's over... You want a confession, I'll give you one. And this you can quote. I've been working on a solo routine.
Stella Liar!
Troop Lousy, yeah, I know. How could I tell you? We still had dates to play.
Stella You sly old sod!
Troop Oh, no, Stella. Joke's on me. You're bailing out first.
Stella Then you owe me a favour.
Troop (*amused*) Don't put money on it.
Stella I need something. For Morganheimer. He wants to see a bit more.
Troop You'll not keep him waiting.
Stella Listen! Not an audition but another side of me, you know.
Troop Don't forget this is arse-end Troop you're talking to.
Stella I never doubted your experience. Taught me a lot, you have. Sorry I wasn't born more grateful... No, something on my own. That's what he wants. And working like we've done so long, a double, well... I haven't got anything.
Troop You've done chorus work.
Stella Years ago.
Troop That was a nice peg-rug you made when we did panto in Huddersfield.
Stella Harry!
Troop What can you do, Stella?
Stella A bloody sight more than you.
Troop Then gerron with it!
Stella I need help.
Troop Sing him *Soulmates*.
Stella A duet on me tod?

Troop rises and picks up the towel. He goes towards the exit L

Harry! Wait!

Troop waits

About the contract. I know I signed it but I never read it. I swear I never read it... I don't know how, Harry... A bloody signature's about all I can manage.
Troop Stuff it, Stella. Never kid a kidder.
Stella God-strike-me-down! Remember the old days when you used to give me a script to learn? Remember? I'd give it back to you, saying I preferred to learn it parrot-fashion?
Troop Good for the act. Made it more spontaneous.
Stella I've spent my life giving printed papers back to people. Headaches, forgot my glasses.
Troop What about all them letters from punters?
Stella Lies, Harry. All part of the performance. Like my bad temper. Stops anyone getting too close and finding out... Never told anyone any of this, Harry Troop, and I wouldn't be telling you now if I didn't need you so much... Got a song my brother wrote. I could do that.

Troop stands resigned as Stella moves C

Honesty, Harry. None of your kidding... If it's not right you've got to say so. I've bared my soul to you, Harry Troop, so the least you can do is give me the benefit of your experience.
Troop Got a routine to polish, Stella.
Stella Please, Harry... And I have got you a present. (*She hurries behind the screen*)
Troop People to see.
Stella (*from behind the screen*) Don't go.

Troop shrugs compliance... Then Stella re-emerges with a square, flat parcel—obviously a picture

Like to have written on it. "To Harry, keeper of my soul". (*She hands the parcel to Troop*) Open it.

Troop removes the brown paper: it's a blow-up photo of him and Stella

That front-of-house picture you liked. I had it glossed and coloured.
Troop Thanks, Stella... Place of honour.
Stella Had it months. Long before the Yank. Didn't know how to give it to you.

Act I   35

Troop I'm grateful.
Stella (*moving* C) Two minutes, Harry, that's all it takes.
Troop Do it… yeah.
Stella No band parts or anything but I can always busk it along. Like you always say, Harry—hit 'em with your courage!

Music Cue No 13. *Stella arranges herself*

All I need now is to forget the bloody words. (*She sings and soft-shoes to* Moon in June)
        How would you like to croon
        A tune about the moon in June
        And spoon upon a swoony honeymoon
        To laze away the day… (*She tails off*)
Troop What's wrong?
Stella Stinks, doesn't it?
Troop No, it's fine. Really.
Stella Not just saying that, are you? I mean, you're ditching me anyway, so what have you got to lose?
Troop You're going to America, Stella. Yank's waiting.
Stella Cold feet, Harry. Not sure I'm up to it… And if Morganheimer's all you say he is——
Troop (*interrupting*) Just cynical old Troopie talking. Hit 'em with your courage, Stella.
Stella (*smiling, reassured*) Yeah… (*she begins soft-shoeing to* Moon In June)
        How would you like to croon
        A tune about the moon in June
        And spoon upon a swoony honeymoon
        To laze away the day
        Upon a sunlit bay
        And stray and play among a sandy dune… (*She tails off*)
Harry?
Troop Stop worrying. Morganheimer'll love it.
Stella No kidding?
Troop No kidding.

Stella smiles at Troop. He smiles reassuringly back

Stella (*resuming her routine*) My heart is a fire of desire
        My head is as light as a balloon
        Your love is all that I require
        So hold me tight and kiss me real soon…
That's it. Just goes on like that.

Pause

Tell me not to go.
Troop Break a leg, Stella. Give my love to Mae West.
Stella God bless you, Harry. (*She blows Troop a kiss*)

Troop smiles and blows a kiss in return

Stella grabs her coat and suitcase, exits R

Troop's smile fades immediately. He looks at the framed picture a moment... Then hurls it savagely at the back wall... He seethes

Music Cue No 14

Black-out

Curtain

ACT II

Lights up on the sitting-room of the nursing home

Music Cue No 15

Troop is seated at the piano, his arms at his sides. The piano lid remains closed. Stephanie is hoovering the carpet

Stephanie He rang last night. Wanted me to let him see Andrew. I reckon the canteen manageress is getting sick of him… Can't be much fun for her, can it? Him harping on about Andrew all the time? Reckon his next move will be to play on my sympathies … beg me to have him back. Tears and regret and admitting what a bloody fool he's been… "Loved you all the time, Stephanie. Took this terrible mistake to make me realize just how much… Can you ever forgive me?" (*She stops work to look at Troop*) Can you play that?
Troop (*rousing and turning*) Eh?
Stephanie The piano.
Troop No.
Stephanie Don't believe you. (*She hoovers again, then stops*) What would you do?
Troop Eh?
Stephanie In my place… I mean, I could never trust him again, could I? While he's crying into his cornflakes it'd be OK—all flowers and "Let me do the washing-up, Stephanie". But give it a year or two and he'd be up to his tricks again. (*She sorts the cushions on Troop's chair*) No… Even if he did want to come back I wouldn't let him. See how he likes being kicked in the teeth.
Troop Thought I was holding all the cards. Won the first few tricks, no trouble. My resentment beating Stella's remorse. Then I played the hurt-pride card. After that the self-pity… Game was in my pocket.

Pause as he goes silent

Stephanie Go on.
Troop Eh?
Stephanie The game was in your pocket.

Troop Ay. Would've thought so… Played my ace, y'see. (*He shakes his head*) Mistake.
Stephanie Your ace?
Troop Hatred… Powerful card, hatred. Revenge isn't a game I'd advise anyone to play. Even when you win you lose. (*He rises and moves past Stephanie*)
Stephanie Are you trying to tell me something?
Troop I'm saying you shouldn't live to regret. If he's not for you, then tell him "no". Don't use the baby to up the ante. Kids condemn you whatever you do… Just keep your decision pure. (*Distracted, he moves upstage to look from the window*)
Stephanie Have you seen the programme for next week?

Troop doesn't respond. Stephanie roots in the pocket of her dress. She produces a piece of paper and scans it

Bingo alternate days… Scrub that—you don't play bingo… Then Tuesday morning there's flower arranging on the veranda.
Troop Flower arranging?
Stephanie Scrub that as well, eh?
Troop No, no. Generates a wild excitement within me, does that. Tell you what, I'll make a wreath and put it in't fridge… Save our Edith some expense… Hey, and put me down for the coffin class, if there is one. Bound to knock one up cheaper than t' Co-op.

Stephanie laughs

Any orgies on the veranda?
Stephanie There's entertainment over in the dayroom. An illusionist. But I'm not supposed to tell you that, it's a secret.

Troop goes quiet again

When are you going to do something for us?
Troop Me?
Stephanie While you're telling me about your career, you could be telling the other residents… Hey! Maybe some of them remember you. That's an idea, you could give a talk. (*She moves towards him*)
Troop On what? (*He moves to his chair*)
Stephanie Harry Troop.
Troop (*sitting*) He's not one for talking at the moment.
Stephanie (*perching on Troop's table*) Only while Harold Burgess lives, right? So we eliminate Harold Burgess. Pinch his notes out of the confidential files and burn them. They'll have to open a new file, titled "Harry Troop"… What d'you think?

Act II

Troop contemplates Stephanie

Troop Would you do that?
Stephanie No.

Troop laughs. Stephanie laughs with him

Did Stella Turner ever make any films?
Troop Fancy having a kip now, if you don't mind. I'll have fish for my dinner.
Stephanie 'Course, I'm forgetting. She couldn't read, could she? Scripts, contracts and all that, would be so much gibberish to her.

Troop sits quietly

Should've known that before she went. Obviously didn't occur to her.
Troop (*sharply*) I've said I'm tired, damn you!
Stephanie Bet it occurred to you.
Troop You're provoking me, young woman. Not good for an old man to be provoked. Matron not told you that?
Stephanie (*rising*) Bottle it then! (*She moves to collect the Hoover*)
Troop There's a cruelty in you, girl.
Stephanie Peddle your lies and delude yourself. And when you get to the Golden Gates, knock with a sponge!
Troop Tongue like a dagger. Sharpen it on your heart, d'you?
Stephanie Everybody's wrong, aren't they?

Music Cue No 16. *"Grey" Edith saunters on from* US, *unseen*

Must be nice to have the monopoly on truth. Old age has done that for you... Had a lot of experience with liars, I have. I married one!

Stephanie goes to the exit L *but Troop has spotted Edith. He reacts apprehensively*

Troop (*to Stephanie*) No! Wait! You're right. Depends who you believe.
Stephanie (*pausing*) Can't guarantee anything till I've heard it, can I?

Edith moves behind Troop as he speaks

Troop Not easy... Each time I try, I get the barrackers in. (*He indicates Edith with a nod of his head*)
Stephanie (*parking the hoover*) Stella Turner. Did you ever see her again?
Troop No.

Edith laughs derisively

I mean, yes.
Stephanie Make your mind up.

Pause as Troop tries to gather thoughts and emotions. Edith moves across to the phone

Troop Cable from America. Said "Arriving Liverpool. Must see you. Stella."
Edith Dictated that over a telephone, didn't she, Dad? For obvious reasons.
Troop I ignored her.
Edith Even though you were playing Liverpool at the time.
Troop At the Empire, yes.
Stephanie (*sitting*) Ah! So she came to see you and you ignored her.
Troop (*confused*) No...
Stephanie Then you saw her.
Edith (*sitting on the piano stool*) You gave instructions at the stage door that she wasn't to be admitted.
Troop She'd left me. Dumped me. Now here she was wanting to pick up the pieces... I was in no mood to listen.
Stephanie Can understand you not being very forgiving but...
Troop (*interrupting*) And who would I be doing it for, eh? Not me. I was doing very well on my own, thank you very much.
Edith Half a dozen lines in a third-rate revue. (*She rises and moves behind Troop*)
Troop More than that. I had pride... Stella should've given me more time. Let me get used to the idea.
Edith (*amused*) Mr Troop now enters a plea of retrospective regret... Won't wash, Dad.
Troop She was headstrong, unmanageable.
Edith And a threat.
Stephanie You managed her OK on stage. You said so.
Edith (*moving in front of Troop*) How long before she'd be grabbing the glory again? Milking the laughs you handed her on a plate? We can all see the lamp burn but who sees the electricity, eh? (*She moves to look from the window*)
Troop It was me that did it. Me! She never understood, just as you don't understand.
Stephanie I understand that she hurt you.

Confused, Troop turns to Stephanie

Troop Eh?

Act II   41

Stephanie And that you gave way to hate... OK, so you ignored her in Liverpool. That was it, was it?
Troop What?
Edith Surely you remember. Raining, you running. A voice calling "Harry". Small face under an umbrella.
Troop (*rising, confused*) No...
Stephanie Oh! So that wasn't it?
Edith (*turning to Troop*) The Crewe Lyceum. You'd just finished. Was going back to your digs.
Troop I'd just finished. Was going back to my digs. She stopped me, we talked. No acrimony.
Stephanie What did you talk about?

Troop shuffles uncomfortably as Edith moves closer

C'mon ... what did you talk about?
Edith Remember it, do you, Dad?
Troop No ... no.
Edith Liar!
Troop All right! Said we could meet for a drink sometime. Not now, I was busy.
Stephanie That all?
Edith But there's more.
Troop There's more, ay. (*He stands a moment, confused between the two women*) Told her to drop me a line when next I was in the North... Left her.
Edith (*ironically*) Drop you a line.
Stephanie Drop you a line?
Troop That's what I said, yes. No acrimony.
Edith But she couldn't write, could she?
Stephanie (*rising*) But she couldn't write, could she? Oh, Mr Troop!
Troop (*emotionally*) Revenge! Holding all the bloody cards but nobody told me suicide were trumps. (*He sobs*)

Stephanie comforts him

Edith saunters off US

(*With effort*) Tablets... She took tablets.
Stephanie Oh no... Well ... well, perhaps she had other problems. Things you didn't know about.
Troop She had nothing. No money, no friends, no hope. I killed her.

Stephanie embraces Troop

Stephanie No, love. People have choice.
Troop I fed her to America knowing she could only fail. I had her soul, y'see. She travelled two thousand miles to get it back... And I played my ace.
Stephanie It was a long time ago, Mr Troop.
Troop No. It were yesterday. Today and tomorrow.

Stephanie assists Troop to the chair and is sitting him down when the phone rings

Stephanie Stay there. Don't move. (*She crosses to the phone and lifts the receiver*) Hallo, residents phone, Havencrest Nursing Home.... (*Bitterly*) What are you doing ringing me here? Who gave you the bloody number? ... Mandy, I know. Well I can't talk even if I wanted to... Sod off! (*She hangs up and returns to Troop*) That was him... Right pair, you and me, eh? At odds with the bloody world.
Troop I want to be Harold Burgess again.
Stephanie Too late for that... I'll kill that Mandy.

Music Cue No 17. *Residents are heard off, breaking into song in the lounge. They're singing* Daisy Bell

Listen to them old fools. Not a care in the world... Senility has its good side, you know... I'll shut out the racket.

Stephanie exits L to shut the door

The song ends abruptly. Troop blows his nose, pulls himself together with effort

Stephanie enters and crosses to him

Troop I'm a nuisance to you.
Stephanie (*behind him*) Say that again! But despite all that, Matron wants me to spend some time with you. On a sort of one-to-one basis.
Troop You mean like sex therapy?
Stephanie That's it, yeah. But without the sex... Hey, guess what I've got in here? (*She goes to the piano, opens the top and removes the scrapbook*) Your scrapbook. Leave it in the office, y'see, and everyone'll have a dekko. Private this is, between you and me. Until such time as I launch you on an unsuspecting public.
Troop Why is it in there?
Stephanie Matron was reading it.
Troop Reading it? In the piano?
Stephanie (*amused*) No.

Act II   43

Troop (*sailing on*) Entrusted to her care and she hides herself away in a bloody piano reading books! How often does this penchant for pianos manifest itself? Do the other residents know?
Stephanie (*amused, moving towards Troop*) Listen... When I came on duty this morning I borrowed it from the office. Hoping you'd let me see it with you... Do you mind?
Troop For whose benefit?
Stephanie Yours.
Troop What's in it for you?
Stephanie Nothing.
Troop Right! Bullshit dispensed with, I'll show you the book.

Stephanie hands the book to Troop then sits on the footstool. Troop dons his glasses and turns the page

I made money, y'know. Invested most of it.
Stephanie (*looking at the book*) That's you as the Deb's Delight... Like the jacket.
Troop The rubber planter made me a shareholder in his building business. He had no business till I staked him. And two bloody cock-eyed ventures before he made anything.
Stephanie (*turning the page*) Hey! There's the fire-eater.
Troop Did I tell you about the rubber planter's motel? Edith talked me into that. (*He quotes Edith*) "Very speculative, Dad, but it'll be a goldmine once they've finished the redevelopment. It'll be near the motorway." Near the motorway, my arse! Was under the bloody motorway when they built it. Only custom they got was drop-in trade when some silly bugger crashed through the barrier!
Stephanie (*amused*) Why do you call him the rubber planter?
Troop He spent time in Malaya.
Stephanie Planting rubber?
Troop No, National Service. Two IC bedding stores. Might have dipped his wick a few times but he didn't plant any bloody rubber.
Stephanie Edith said you were one for feeding prejudices.
Troop Thought you wanted to see the book.
Stephanie She struck me as OK.
Troop Got me down for Old Nick's bonfire she has. (*He gets suspicious, closes the book*) What's she been telling you? Mention her mother?
Stephanie What if she did?

Tense, Troop removes his glasses

OK, forget the book. Do it another time. (*She rises and moves* L) Still got the linen cupboard to sort anyway. (*She makes to exit*)

Troop Well, if you'd rather be among the sheets and pillowcases.

Stephanie, unseen by Troop, smiles, and returns to him

Stephanie (*taking the book*) Tell me about the Great Krakatoa.
Troop Big fella. Came to us from circus. Fire-eater, sword swallower.
Stephanie I know that. What else?
Troop We used to send him round with the Arris.
Stephanie The what?
Troop Aristotle—bottle. That's how we used to take collections. With a bottle. Wide enough for cash but you couldn't dip into it.
Stephanie Was this on the pier?
Troop Summer work was all piers if you wasn't a top liner. By that time I'd kicked the Deb's Delight into touch. It was dated, y'see.

Stephanie unfolds a longer piece of paper that's attached to a page of the book

Stephanie Hey! What's this?
Troop When I worked with Krakatoa I did second comic and sketch routines.
Stephanie (*reading*) "I have a set menu at my establishment. Kippers Monday, Tuesday and Wednesday. Bloaters Thursday and Friday."
Troop What?
Stephanie That's what it says. (*She unfolds the papers concertina-fashion*) It's a sketch. Let's do it... Are you ready?
Troop Ready for what?
Stephanie C'mon, Mr Troop. It's like swimming. You never really forget. (*She reads*) "Enter Jessie as seaside landlady."
Troop Jessie...

Music Cue No 18. *Two musical phrases then atmosphere*

Stephanie (*reading*) "I have a set menu at my establishment. Kippers Monday, Tuesday and Wednesday. Bloaters Thursday and Friday."
Troop What about weekends?
Stephanie (*reading*) "That's a surprise."
Troop I hope it's the bloody butcher!

Stephanie laughs

Jessie (*echoing off*) Keep your rooms Christian. No gambling, swearing or alcohol.

Act II

Stephanie loses her place in the sketch

Troop (*quietly*) Jessie?
Jessie (*echoing off*) Two pounds a week all found.
Troop What about women?
Stephanie (*scanning quickly, then reading*) "You'll have to find your own." (*To Troop*) Don't go so quick.
Troop Do you take cheques?
Jessie (*echoing off*) Take anyone that flushes the lav and doesn't leave a ring round the bath.

Troop laughs

Stephanie (*excited, back to Troop*) You and me could do this. Next week after flower arranging... I'm going to tell Matron. And don't say "no", because I'm not listening.
Troop Are the rooms bug-free?
Jessie (*echoing, off*) Free? What d'you think this is, gift week?

Troop laughs but Stephanie is busy trying to follow the text

Stephanie (*finding her place*) "You want 'em free, mate, you should've gone to Thora Plunkett's behind the gasworks!"
Troop (*amused*) Oh dear, oh dear...
Stephanie I'll improve. That's if you don't mind working with amateurs. (*She replaces the book under the piano lid*)
Jessie (*echoing off*) Good crowd out there today, Harry. What was the Arris?
Troop Should clear twenty quid at least.
Stephanie (*moving to the exit* L) Won't get paid, Mr Troop. We'll be doing it for love... I'll tell Matron now before you change your mind.

Stephanie exits L *with the hoover*

The Lights go down on the sitting-room. Troop rises. He removes his dressing-gown to reveal a silk dressing-gown beneath... He bounds into the dressing-room area and it lights simultaneously

Troop opens the door to greet Jessie who enters wearing a pierrot outfit

Troop Jessie! Come in, love.
Jessie Ever find yourself counting heads?
Troop Theirs or ours? (*He pours drinks*) C'mon, Jessie love. Have a drop of this.

Jessie You're corrupting me, Harry Troop. Inviting me to your dressing-room for an immoral purpose.
Troop No such thing! (*He hands Jessie a glass of beer*)
Jessie Spoilsport! (*She sits on the trunk*)
Troop (*pouring beer for himself*) Been meaning to ask what your plans are. For after the season.
Jessie Back home to Stepney. Just hope Mum's found me a job. What about you?
Troop Waiting on my agent. He's listening out for anyone who wants a partner. Leaving it late, though.
Jessie You'll make out, Harry. Who was it said Harry Troop's the best feed in the business?
Troop Sounds like my agent!
Jessie (*amused*) But that's the trouble with this game. Forever beholden to other people. Old Kraky's asked me to give him a hand, actually. You know I've been seeing quite a bit of him lately.
Troop It's work, Jessie.
Jessie I know. But I don't fancy circus, Harry. All that sawdust and sealion shit.

Troop laughs

And old Kraky's not the most stable bloke I've ever walked out with. Never seen anyone shift it like he does.
Troop (*raising his glass*) They call it the sword-swallower's gargle.
Jessie That's why they trust him with the Arris. Last bottle he dropped was out of his soddin' pram!

Troop is amused

No, I can't see me taking to it. Me in tutu and tights, old Kracky lit up like a bleedin' pinwheel.
Troop You're funny, you know that?
Jessie How d'you mean?
Troop Genuinely funny... Have you thought about you and me getting together?
Jessie Is that proposal or proposition, Harry Troop?
Troop Which would you prefer?
Jessie Well, when you don't get that many offers you're not that particular.
Troop (*moving to Jessie*) What would Mother say?
Jessie Marry the geezer and make it proper.
Troop Mum's a moralist. (*He refills her glass*)
Jessie No, an economist. Why book two rooms when you can get away with one.

Act II   47

Troop Devise a few routines and I might get us a tour on the Broadhead. (*He sits on the trunk*)

Jessie If I'm going to take you on, Harry Troop, there's a few things I want straight. I do the domestics and you do the business. And we use the King's English as a means o' communication.

Troop (*toasting*) I'll drink to that.

Jessie Then what the bleedin' 'ell are you on about?

Troop The Broadhead circuit up North. My name's still good and they'll give us a try. What d'you say?

Jessie I'm no Stella Turner.

Troop Why mention Stella?

Jessie Well, I've heard a lot about her. Nobody's going to snap Jessie Lester up and whip her off to America. Like it or not, Stella was one hell of a performer.

Troop So everyone keeps telling me.

Jessie Funny. The only bloke I've never heard mensh is yourself. Still, you're not one for flashin' your foreskin at a Bar Mitzvah, are you, love? Quiet as a Scotch auction you are, and no mistake.

Troop Stoic Northern reticence.

Jessie Not got Stella's voice.

Troop Let's forget Stella, eh, Jessie? (*He moves to the dressing-table*)

Jessie Just tellin' you I can't sing. Comes out with a sort o' skin over it... Well, what do you expect when you train on Woodbines? (*She rises and moves to Troop*) And another thing, my dancing's nowt to write home about.

Troop Why write home? (*He drinks*)

Jessie Tell Mum I'm getting wed next week.

Troop (*spluttering on the beer*) Next week?

Jessie Well, I need time to get my bottom drawer together, don't I? (*She moves to the door*) And I'll tell you somethin' else, Harry Troop. This is one show you're going into without a rehearsal.

Jessie blows him a kiss and exits

Troop (*amused; moving to the door after Jessie*) Jessie! Jessie! (*He returns amused to the dressing-table*) What a girl! Tell Mum I'm getting married next week. (*He tops up his glass*) She's a scream. (*He drinks and thinks*) She wouldn't... Would she? She bloody would!

Troop darts off

(*Off; loudly*) Jessie!

Black-out

Then wedding bells are heard... Music becomes The Wedding March *and a spot lights Jessie and Troop standing with their backs to the audience... Then music* (**Music Cue No 19**) *into* Jessie's Tango

Jessie moves in sultry fashion to the music, a rose between her teeth or held in her waving hand. Troop tangos too, but each time he attempts to close with Jessie he meets with some disaster. Her flamboyant gestures catch him awkwardly; hand across the face; rose in his mouth; foot on his toe; accidental kick in the privates... Final trip has Troop being ejected into the wings... Jessie dances on. Troop staggers back but Jessie stamps on his toe. He manages to grab Jessie's hand but is tumbled judo-style. Number ends with Jessie standing tempestuously on prostrate Troop...

Black-out

Troop and Jessie are heard in voice-over

Jessie (*v/o*) Blimey, Harry, I'm knackered.
Troop (*v/o*) We'll not be doing it much longer, anyway. Oh, and I've cancelled summer season. I don't want you throwing yourself about. Not in your condition.
Jessie (*v/o*) Just my luck to get pregnant when things were lookin' up... Why didn't you use somethin'?
Troop (*v/o*) What d'you think I've been using?
Jessie (*v/o*) I meant precautions. Mum said I should never have married a foreigner.
Troop (*v/o*) Foreigner?
Jessie (*v/o*) Communications, Harry. Remember? The King's English? When I say "Wotcha cock" I mean it literally... Watch it! Know what I mean? I do wish you'd listen.

Amused, Troop moves into the dressing-room with Jessie. He carries a towel

Troop That's the trouble, love. Too many listening nowadays. Wireless is killing trade.
Jessie Don't fret, Harry. There'll always be stages. Somewhere for you and me.

Troop hugs her affectionately. The Light changes as Jessie takes the towel from Troop and goes behind the screen... I Wanna Be Happy *is played low and slow... We're back in the sitting-room*

(*Echoing off*) Come back hungry for what we have to give 'em...

Act II   49

During the following, Troop, now wearing a cardigan, enters the sitting-room and shuffles to the piano

There'll always be somewhere, love… Somewhere for you and me.

Music Cue No 20. *Troop sits contemplating the closed piano lid*

Stephanie enters L

Stephanie I've got good news and bad news. Which d'you want first?
Troop Eh?
Stephanie The good news or the bad news? Which d'you want first?
Troop (*rising*) I'm not partick.
Stephanie (*disappointed*) The illusionist can't come.
Troop (*moving past Stephanie*) What's the bad news?

Stephanie, hands on hips, gives Troop an old-fashioned look as he moves towards the window

Stephanie Everyone's disappointed. Including me. I was looking forward to seeing him.
Troop Have a job now, won't you? Probably vanished himself and forgot the rest of the trick.
Stephanie Car trouble, he reckons. Got all these cabinets and things. Can't very well bring them on the bus, can he? Matron's schedule's gone kaput with him not coming… But I haven't told you the good news. Already got a replacement. Matron likes the sketch idea.
Troop What sketch idea?
Stephanie Oh, c'mon, you weren't kiddin' me, were you? You're not backing out?

Troop looks blank as Stephanie moves to the piano

Y'know… "Enter Jessie as seaside landlady". (*She removes the scrapbook from the piano top*)
Troop Oh no. Jessie can't perform. Not in her condition. If they want me they can have me, but I'm a solo. Tell 'em that. And you can tell 'em as well that I don't do auditions.

Pause

Stephanie (*moving towards Troop*) You're back with the fairies again, aren't you? And I've opened my big mouth to Matron.

Troop That's the secret, y'see. Make out you're not bothered and they break their necks to get you.
Stephanie This one-to-one's not working, is it? I'm by myself but there's about three or four of you.
Troop That's how I cracked it with wireless.
Stephanie Can I be frank, Mr Troop? You're pissing me right off! (*Fed-up, she plonks herself in his chair*)
Troop We saw radio as a gimmick to begin with. A nine-days' wonder. Then it gradually took on more importance. Broadcasting brought status. Put you further up the bill and improved the money... A few made the transition but a lot got lost on the way... There's a tale about a fella who worked doves. Y'know, a magician. Didn't get a bookin' in years. One day his agent sent him a telegram. "Have got you split-week Halifax." Fella wired back... "Too late. Have eaten act."

Stephanie laughs

Music Cue No 21. *Troop looks from the window as "grey" Edith saunters on from* US

I don't tell it as a joke.
Stephanie Oh, I am sorry! Shave my head and tighten my chastity belt!
Edith Telling porkies again, Dad?

Troop reacts. He spots Edith

Troop (*aware of Edith*) I managed. Even without Jessie, I managed... Harry Troop, front-cloth comic versus the arbiters of good taste and morality.
Edith You were never a comic, Dad. You were Mum's feed.
Troop Ay! I fed and I bled but that's not enough, is it? What more can I give but my regret. (*He sobs*) My sorrow... I loved her.
Edith I needed her.

Upset, Troop wipes away tears. Stephanie rises from the chair to embrace him

Stephanie OK, don't panic. We'll do it some other time.
Troop (*savage, shrugging her away*) Be old yourself one day. It'll be my turn. I'll be up there waiting for you.
Stephanie Then maybe we'll do it then.
Troop (*appealing to Stephanie*) I had a greatness in me.
Stephanie I know. And I'm Florence Nightingale!
Edith Others made the transition. You said so yourself. Why not Harry Troop? But the monkey needed the organ-grinder, didn't he?

Act II 51

Edith exits US *laughing*

Troop Edith! Edith! Listen to me!
Stephanie Christ! Mr Troop! Edith's miles away.
Troop Miles off, y'mean. Any daughter would be proud.

The phone rings. Troop *beats Stephanie to it*

(*Into the phone*) Jessie? ... Jessie?
Stephanie Give it here! (*She wrestles the receiver off Troop—then bitterly into the phone*) Look, I've told you... (*Softer*) Oh, it's you. ... No, some old fella. One of the residents.
Troop Tell her I did my best.
Stephanie (*into the phone*) Can't talk now, Mandy... Is he OK?
Troop Didn't get a chance to do the act. Wasn't an audition, more a bloody execution... Here, let me tell her. (*He tries to grab the phone off Stephanie*)
Stephanie (*narked*) Gerroff!

Troop shuffles sadly away

(*Into the phone*) Have to go. (*She hangs up. She watches the silent Troop a moment*)
Troop I'm Northern, aren't I?
Stephanie Yeah. And crackers!
Troop Played the North. My own kind. Bloody sure I wasn't going to change my way of talkin' just to suit them.
Stephanie (*disinterested*) No.
Troop The BBC... Should've seen 'em. Toffee-nosed graduates, all puffin' du Mauriers and slaverin' down their Fair Isle pullovers. Corduroys, cravats, birds done up like Bertrand bloody Russell. (*Loudly*) Wankers!
Stephanie Keep your voice down. Matron'll hear you.
BBC Woman (*echoing off*) Can't blame the BBC for wanting to establish a standard speech pattern. A language preferred and clearly understood.
Troop (*volubly*) Bollocks!
Stephanie (*towards him*) Quiet! You'll get me in trouble, you will... No more swearing, right?
Troop Of course not, no. One forgets one's self. One will treat the BBC with a reverence usually associated with black crêpe and embalming fluid. One will observe the proprieties.
Stephanie Promise?
Troop (*moving towards exit* R) On time, best bib and tucker, act as known. No deviation. (*He moves to exit* L) I'm going for a pee.

Troop exits

Stephanie Will you be OK? I'll give you five minutes.
Troop (*off; calling*) Take me that long to find it!

The Lights go off on the sitting-room as Stephanie goes off after Troop

The Lights come up

An austere BBC Woman is on stage. She wears horn-rimmed spectacles and has headphones round her neck. She carries a clipboard and script in one hand and an old BBC stand microphone in the other

She puts the microphone DS

BBC Woman (*into the microphone*) Connected at my end... Anyone out there? Monica here... Ah! Good morning, Peter. (*She listens*) Oh, it's not Peter, it's Jeremy. Never mind, it's still a good morning... All set are we?

Static whine that makes her cringe

Thank you, Jeremy!

Troop, in a suit, enters from the wings

Good morning. Not nervous, are we? (*She hands Troop a script*) Little memory refresher before we start.
Troop (*scanning the script*) It's my act.
BBC Woman (*retrieving the script from Troop*) The guttural vowel sounds of your native North have a certain rustic charm, of course. Similarly the burr of the West Country. Both, however, are verbal impracticalities, bred in ignorance and reared in isolation. They shall be replaced by a definitive English. Not through any force we can exert but though example... A brief word of warning. So many of the music-hall fraternity tend to underestimate the massive potential of broadcasting... Finally, we are the invited guests of our listeners and need to behave accordingly.

She positions Troop in front of the microphone and fits headphones to her ears

(*Into the microphone*) Sounds levels, Jeremy... This is the... (*To Troop*) I'm sorry, I've forgotten your name.
Troop Troop. Harry Troop.
BBC Woman (*into the microphone*) This is the Harry Troop audition. Testing for levels ... one-two, buckle my shoe. Three-four, knock at the door... OK? Fine.

Act II

BBC Woman again adjusts Troop to a very specific point in front of the microphone

    In your own time, Mr Troop. Stay close and don't shout.
Troop Just here?
BBC Woman There. In your own time.
Troop I can start?
BBC Woman Please.

She again adjusts Troop's position. She gives a quick beam of encouragement to uncomfortable Troop

Troop Good evening, good evening, good evening. A very funny thing happened to me on my way to the theatre tonight——
BBC Woman *(interrupting)* Stop! Sorry... erm... You needn't move about so much. Conversational level. Consistent tone... Go on.
Troop Good evening, good evening, good evening. A very funny thing happened to me on my way to the theatre tonight. Coalman's horse dropped dead right in the middle of the tramlines——
BBC Woman *(interrupting)* You're performing, Mr Troop. Save your energy. It isn't necessary, believe me... Poor Jeremy's having an awful time with his knobs.

She fixes Troop to that very specific position again

Troop Start again?
BBC Woman By all means.
Troop Right... Good evening, good evening——
BBC Woman *(interrupting)* No, no, we needn't go through all that again. We know about the dead horse.
Troop *(aside)* So do I, I'm floggin' it!
BBC Woman Sorry?
Troop Nothing... Carry on, do I?
BBC Woman Of course... It's lovely.
Troop I'm obliged... Anyway, a copper comes over with his notebook. Y'now, PC Plod from the Backward Squad. "Ey, up!" he sez, licking his pencil, "Where are we?" "Piccadilly," sez the coalman. "Can't spell that," sez the copper. "Help me drag it round the corner into Tib Street."
BBC Woman *(moving Troop)* Excuse me a moment. *(Into the microphone)* Something like "Hey up", Jeremy love. Northern colloquial but clear enough from my end... Say again ... erm... "Help me drag it round the corner into Tib Street". *(She turns to Troop for confirmation)*

Troop nods agreement

Jeremy... Jeremy! Love... I'll judge the material, you judge the sound reproduction. (*To Troop*) If you'd care to continue, Mr Troop.

Troop moves back to the microphone. Another positional adjustment

That's fine... And you're very funny. Try to relax. That's it.
Troop Just been on holiday, actually...
BBC Woman (*interrupting*) It's about stillness, Mr Troop.
Troop Yes. (*He is getting stiller by the second*)

BBC Woman beams encouragement

On holiday... to Southport... Took the wife... Well you always pack stuff you don't need, don't you? Got terrible digs. Landlady used to put the gravy on the railway line for the trains to slice. One night she did Ham Surprise. I didn't get any. I sez, "Where's mine?" She sez, "You're gettin' none. How d'yer feel?" I sez, "I'm surprised". She sez, "That's what it sez on the menu!" (*He steps back*) I'm sorry, I can't work like this. Can't I just do the act and learn the technique later?
BBC Woman I'm afraid we haven't time for that. And the technique is the act. Control your natural way of working and direct your energies through the instrument of your voice... I don't mean to be offensive when I say our appeal is to a slightly more discerning audience than the one you're used to.
Troop That's interesting. Might one ask if they have the usual bodily functions?
BBC Woman Mind-pictures, Mr Troop. Substance from the amorphous.
Troop I do apologise. I was labouring under the delusion that I was here to make people laugh.
BBC Woman Relax, keep still, and enunciate clearly and precisely.
Troop Oh dear, I haven't enunciated since Nanny bought me the boxing gloves. (*He puts his hand in his pocket*) All right if I just jangle my small change? (*He rattles the change in his pocket by way of demonstration*)
BBC Woman Substance, Mr Troop.
Troop From the amorphous.
BBC Woman Exactly.
Troop Well, if it's substance you want, you can have it... Is Jeremy plugged in?
BBC Woman All set to go... Ah!

She carefully positions Troop at the microphone

I hope you'll forgive my constant attention to position.

Act II   55

Troop Not at all. You do have a certain lightness of touch I am learning to appreciate.

BBC Woman moves away

Ready?
BBC Woman When you are, Mr Troop.
Troop Hang on to your cat's whisker, Jeremy, this is subtle stuff... Must tell you about my mate, Jack. Funny fella... Caught him the other day putting flour on his old man. There he was, two-pound bag, sprinklin' it all over his silent member. I said, "Is it self-raising?" He sez, "Well, I don't need a block and tackle!"

BBC woman tries to find the gag on the clipboard. Troop picks up the microphone and moves, playing the audience. The spotlight follows him

Well-hung fella is Jack. Round-shouldered and has these special shoes fitted. But his wife's got a lot to put up with. (*To a specific point in the audience*) No, love, I mean apart from that.

BBC Woman attempts to wrestle the microphone from the oblivious Troop

If you're going to tell your own jokes it was a waste o' time me coming! Well, don't vote on it for Godsake!

Finally BBC Woman manages to wrestle the microphone from Troop and hurries off quickly with it

Troop carries on regardless, addressing the audience in general again

No, seriously, Jack's missis has got her problems. Tellin' me only yesterday... Can't stand ironing, hates dusting and the lodger's getting on top of her!

Music Cue No 22

Black-out

Music Cue No 23

The Lights come up on the sitting-room

Stephanie enters L with a vase of flowers which she places on the occasional table. She also carries a radio cassette player

She is arranging flowers as Troop shuffles on R

Stephanie Good morning. Still alive, then?

Unresponsive, Troop passes her

Never mind, can't have everything... Good news and not-so good news this time. Are you ready for this?

Troop doesn't respond

Hey! I'm talking to you.
Troop The BB-bloody-C! I didn't die, y'know. I was done to death. That lot couldn't spot a joke if it grabbed 'em by the knackers... Wireless! (*He sits in his chair*)
Stephanie Funny you should say that. (*She brings the radio cassette from the table*)
Troop And some of the comics they used ... uh! Remember Stainless Stephen, d'yer?
Stephanie Before my time, I think.
Troop About as funny as gettin' your leg trapped! And Harry Hemsley. My God! If he was a comic, the Boston strangler was a physiotherapist!

Stephanie produces a tape cassette from her pocket

Stephanie Enough of your painful past. Brace yourself—you're coming up to date. (*She fits the cassette into the recorder*)
Troop Took a war to convince 'em I was funny. Other side, y'see, had all the big names. Hitler, Goebbels, Ribbentrop. All playing to packed houses. As war is more palpable than cerebral, more arse than head, they gave me another chance.
Stephanie (*pressing the play button*) Listen.
Troop Not Stainless Stephen?
Stephanie Listen! (*She sits on the stool*)
Toby (*on tape*) Hallo, Gramps. Toby speaking. Feel a bit silly talking to a machine but it's Mum's idea. Said it might cheer you up. Anyway, how are you? Things are a bit hectic here. Mum may have told you that I'm articled to a solicitor. Didn't know there was so much reading and studying involved... Anyway, look forward to seeing you when the pressure's off. Meanwhile, take care, eh? Bye for now, Gramps.

Troop sits silent. Stephanie watches him

Act II   57

Stephanie See! You're not forgotten. And I know your name for sure now... It's Gramps.
Ben (*on tape*) Hiya, Gramps. Ben speaking. Intended coming with Mum next weekend but school's organised a trip to Spain. It's part of the A-level syllabus so I can't miss it... Erm ... that's all really... Look after yourself... Bye.
Stephanie (*rising to press the stop button*) Your grandkids. Now wasn't that nice? (*She removes the cassette and puts it on the table*) They'll turn up when you least expect it.
Troop I tried to get there... I tried.
Stephanie Get where?
Troop For my Mam... She'll not forgive me and no reason she should.
Stephanie Why can't you relax, Mr Troop? Enjoy the moment?

Music Cue No 24

A distant strain of Salvation Army music from Act I

Troop Was doing that in Scarborough the day she died. Day they buried her I had a matinee... The moment came and went. (*Loudly*) Wanted you to be proud o' me!
Stephanie (*going to him*) She was, I'm sure.
Troop Second comic wasn't good enough for you, Mam. You deserved glory. Flash car in the street. Folk nudgin' each other and saying "That's Winnie Burgess's lad. Done well for himself." (*He chokes on emotion*) I couldn't come back. I wasn't ready.

Salvation Army music fades

Stephanie (*putting her arm around Troop*) Oh, c'mon, not waterworks again. Edith's proud of you. And the lads.
Troop Ay...
Stephanie Play your tape again?
Troop If you like.
Stephanie (*pressing the start button*) Great!

Stephanie exits L

Troop sits distracted

BBC Announcer (*on tape*) This is the BBC Light Programme. May I remind you that at two o'clock this afternoon you can hear *The Radio Doctor*. This will be followed by a repeat of a programme first broadcast last Friday featuring Ambrose and his orchestra. But now it's over to Bill Gates and a factory somewhere in England for *Workers' Playtime.*

Music Cue No 25. *Community singing from the cassette—last few bars of* Side by Side. *Then applause, whistles from the recorded audience*

BBC Announcer 2 (*on tape*) Our first guests appear by kind permission of the Ministry of Laughter. A warm welcome for those Comedy Fusiliers, Harry Troop and Jessie!

Music Cue No 26

Opening bars of Comedy Fusiliers. *Troop reacts*

Jessie (*on tape*) I don't know where I am, Harry. Where are we?

Panicky Troop reaches over to the cassette. It clatters to the floor and breaks

Troop gets to his feet as Stephanie hurries on from L

Stephanie What's the matter now? (*She spots the wreckage*) Oh no!
Troop (*moving towards the exit* R) Nothin'... Everythin's fine.
Stephanie (*gathering the wrecked recorder*) Looks like it, doesn't it?
Troop Go on. About your business.
Stephanie Sit down, before you wreck the place.
Troop (*heading for the exit*) I'm coming, Jessie... Got the props?

Troop exits

Stephanie (*going after Troop with the wrecked recorder*) Mr Troop!

Stephanie exits after him

The Lights go down on the sitting-room... Air-raid siren is heard. Searchlight scans the stage and audience

Jessie comes on stage in the darkness, holding a night-light in a jam jar

The searchlight goes off. Siren fades

Music Cue No 27. *Opening bars of* Comedy Fusiliers

Jessie (*in the darkness*) I don't know where I am, Harry. Where are we?

Act II   59

Troop (*off*) A factory somewhere in England.
Jessie Lot o' use that is, mate. I'm still in the dark.
Troop (*off*) They make ball-bearings.
Jessie D'they? Well I've lost me bearings, Harry. How d'you feel?

The Lights come up on stage

    Troop enters and joins Jessie

They wear battle dress tops, tin hats and carry rifles... Troop and Jessie sing
Comedy Fusiliers

Jessie and Troop Our regiment has only two.
                You're lookin' at the pair.
                There's no-one else apart from us
                To line up on the square
                When the sergeant sez form threes
                We scratch our heads in doubt
                All we can do is bluff it through
                And walk about spread out.

Troop and Jessie simulate "walkin' about spread out" as music "da-das"
before chorus

                We all love you, Sergeant Major
                We'll prove it by standin' you some beers
                We all love you, Sergeant Major
                Just love us back. Give us the sack
                The Comedy Fusiliers.

The rhythm continues

Jessie (*to the audience*) Hey! Did you know my mate Harry's protectin' Buckin'am Palace? He is! Not on his own, mind. There's him and a few more sandbags!

They sing Comedy Fusiliers *again*

Jessie and Troop We were called up by mistake
                To fight this flippin' war
                We didn't pass no medical
                In fact we're not quite sure
                What we are a doin' here

            And no-one else is either
            We'd rather be in Civvy Street
            And cut out all the mither!

            Please send us home, Quartermaster
            Before we soak our battledress in tears
            Please send us home, Quartermaster
            Just rubber stamp
            And we'll decamp
            The Comedy Fusiliers...

The rhythm continues

Jessie Ain't much good at this guard duty, Harry. Never know what to do.
Troop Don't worry, I'll teach you. (*He points out over the audience*) Look out there from ten o'clock to two o'clock.
Jessie Oh right, Harry, ta...

Troop looks out but casual Jessie yawns, leans on her rifle and examines her nails. Troop notices this

Troop Why aren't you looking?
Jessie (*glancing at her watch*) It's only quarter-to-nine.
Troop (*grabbing Jessie*) Come here! Rifle at the ready. Covering over there to over there. (*He gets the rifle to Jessie's shoulder and moves her in an arc over the audience*) That's known as your arc of fire.
Jessie Hark at what, Harry?
Troop Fire, you fool, fire!

Drum shop signifies Jessie loosing off bullet. Both stagger back in recoil... Then into song again

Jessie and Troop When we were in the desert
            We had this bright idea
            To wear our tunics back-to-front
            And trousers front-to-rear.
            The Panzers did a quick retreat
            As we scarpered from the fray
            They all took short
            'Cos Rommel thought
            We were coming Hitler's way.

            Please send us home, grateful Nation

Act II

> We said tarrah to Monty in Algiers
> Please send us home, grateful Nation
> We did our stuff
> And that's enough
> The Comedy Fusiliers...

The rhythm continues

Troop Thing I can't stand, Jessie, is the bull.
Jessie Don't know, Harry. The Sergeant Major's always been very nice to me. Takes me in his office and gives me drill practice.
Troop How do you know it's drill practice?
Jessie Well after we've finished he always says, "Right! Dress!"
Troop You want to be very careful, Jessie. You can be cashiered for that. They strip you of your decorations.
Jessie Blow that! I always like to keep my earrings on, Harry... Battle honours they are, mate. Battle honours!

Into the song again

Jessie and Troop Our regiment has only two
> You're lookin' at the pair
> The army's not the place for us
> We'd rather be elsewhere
> The cookhouse tea was made BC
> The grub's no appetiser
> There's rissoles there
> With snow-white hair
> That fought against the Kaiser!
>
> Please send us home, Mr Churchill
> We'll send cigars as grateful souvenirs
> Please send us home, Mr Churchill
> Just make the sign (*They show victory fingers*)
> And we'll resign
> The Comedy ... Comedy ... Comedy ... Comedy Fusiliers!

Troop and Jessie salute

Black-out

Music Cue No 28

The Lights grow slowly on the sitting-room

Stephanie is in Troop's chair, smoking. Troop, in dressing-gown, is seated at the piano, his arms at his sides. The lid is down

Stephanie Matron reckons I've got staff-nurse potential... She should know. Worked at a garage before her husband set her up in this place. (*She contemplates Troop*) Open the lid. Go on, open it.
Troop Eh?
Stephanie Play the piano. Tinkle. I'll have it moved, if you like. Put it on the veranda. Flower arranging to music. Save on the comb and paper. (*She pauses*) Open that and we might open you.
Troop (*rising*) Hear that, did you? The Comedy Fusiliers? How could I turn my back on all that laughter? It dragged me. Like a magnet.
Stephanie (*removing the cassette from her pocket*) You heard a bit of this then? That why you smashed the recorder?
Troop Clever that. You and Edith concoct it between you? Tell her it brought back sadness beyond tears.
Stephanie At least sadness is an honest emotion. You can kid your head but never your heart... Want a fag?
Troop (*moving to the window*) No. I'm opposed to all forms of self-abuse. Drugs, masturbation, amateur dramatics.

Stephanie can't resist laughing

Laugh if you want to, it won't go to my head. I've made cats laugh.
Stephanie Muddlecombe?
Troop (*at the window*) He's dead. They're all dead. I'm dead. Been dead for years. It killed me like it killed... (*He checks himself*) I just kept on breathing, that's all.
Stephanie Killed who?

No response from Troop

Stella Turner? I know about her... Did Jessie retire?

Troop moves towards his chair. Stephanie vacates it and pummels cushions

Troop (*sitting*) Like having a devil inside you ... living off your optimism, your ambition... The light always beckoning, promising. An addiction.
Stephanie Was Jessie addicted? (*She sits on the stool by Troop*)
Troop Rainbow chasing... Truth was, I was no good on my own. Look at me now, eh. Can't even make a decent stab at dying.
Stephanie It's not time. You're not at peace. (*She pauses*) Can I ask a favour?
Troop It's finished now. It's over. You mean well, I know you do, and you get credit for that. But there's no more remembering. Hurts too much.

Act II

Stephanie Tell me about the end.
Troop (*giving her the tape from the table*) Memory tape's full. Ready for the rewinding.
Stephanie Not quite. Tell me about you and Jessie.
Troop You've heard. Did our bit for the war effort.
Stephanie What happened?
Troop We won. Beat Hitler.
Stephanie (*rising and moving to the piano*) Love to be there when Saint Peter reads out your CV. Might solve a mystery or two. (*She watches Troop. Then she opens the piano lid and tinkles three one-finger notes at random*)

Troop is immersed in his own thoughts

Did you and Jessie just stop?
Troop No... But I could've stopped her. Kidded myself it was doing her good. She used to say, "What else would I be doing if I wasn't doing this? Stop fussing, Harry." Why didn't she tell me?

Music Cue No 29

The Light is dimming slowly on Troop and Stephanie. Footstep Poetry *is heard played low and slow*

Stephanie Tell you what?
Troop Why did she go on giving? Maybe she did tell me and I didn't listen.
Stephanie We're all chasing rainbows, Mr Troop. All following the light. Jessie went where her light shone brightest. Her choice.
Troop (*rising and shuffling towards exit* L) Silent to the last she was. Every night I'd ask her. "Are you all right, Jessie, love?" Every night.

Troop exits R

The Lights come up on stage wings and Jessie in a ball gown ready for Footstep Poetry. *She holds the rail and gasps for breath*

Jessie Stop fussin', Harry, and watch the conductor's stick. He's not wavin' it about to keep the bleedin' flies off, y'know. Last night you finished a length an' half in front of everybody else!
Troop (*off*) I'm worried about your breathing. All that gravel on your chest.
Jessie Stop fussin'... It's nothing Dr Footlights can't put right. (*She moves* C *and sings*)
        We can tap our feet
        And make a melody complete with harmony

>   Give us the chance to dance
>   And we'll make footstep poetry.
>   Just move in the shoes
>   And a little muscle,
>   Can rustle up the music of the birds.
>   We can say
>   In one neat chassé
>   What Shakespeare conveyed in all his words.
>
>   Watch us move a joint
>   And counterpoint it with a bedtime nursery rhyme
>   Combine a heel and toe
>   And hear it flow on so sublime.
>   See what that old
>   Soft-shoe can do
>   The sweeter the meter so we
>   Can tonight write footstep poetry...

Troop comes on in top hat and tails to croon **Waltz Around the Floor** *as Jessie harmonises to melody*

Troop   Maybe my baby
            Will let me waltz her once around the floor
Jessie We'll make such harmony...
Troop   Hold her near and whisper clear
            And tell her she's the one girl I adore.
Jessie With our footstep poetry...
Troop   Her eyes are lit with paradise
            Her smile so nice it makes my heartstrings sing
Jessie The music of the birds...
Troop   She's definitely the one for me
            And hopefully I'll hear those church bells ring...

Jessie staggers, hangs on to Troop. She becomes increasingly distressed during the following

>   She's my pie in the sky
>   The apple of my eye
>   The one girl that I'm waiting for
>   So baby, I'm saying maybe,
>   She'll let me waltz her once around the floor.

Jessie staggers into the wings and off

Act II   65

Troop, though concerned, carries on. His singing done, he soft-shoes Waltz
Around the Floor *reprise. Typical "show must go on" performance*

Little Edith (*little girl voice on tape*) Daddy? Daddy?
Troop (*dancing*) What is it, pet?
Little Edith (*on tape*) It's my birthday, Daddy. I'm having a party.
Troop (*dancing*) Not forgotten, love. Your present should arrive on the day... Nanna Lester looking after you, is she?
Little Edith (*on tape*) She sends her love. I do understand, honest I do... But I'm frightened, Daddy.
Troop (*dancing on*) Nothing to be frightened of, pet. Don't worry.
Little Edith (*on tape*) Mummy went away and never came back... When are you coming home?
Troop (*moving away in the spot*) Soon... Very soon... So many people relying on me, pet. You wouldn't want your daddy letting them down, now would you?

No response—Edith has gone

Edith? Edith? (*He dances on*)
Edith (*mature voice on tape*) I'm getting married, Dad.
Troop (*dancing*) Congratulations... Do I know him?
Edith (*on tape*) You met briefly at Nanna Lester's funeral... Stop a minute and listen.
Troop (*dancing on*) Nature of the business, you know that. You don't walk off, you sneak off when nobody's looking... My turn'll come.
Edith (*on tape*) We're trying to fix a date. We thought July.
Troop (*dancing*) Height of the season.
Edith (*on tape*) You will be there, won't you? To give me away.

The tunes are gradually being layered one on the other—Soulmates, Comedy Fusiliers, *etc. Troop is having difficulty stepping as Lights begin flashing*

Troop (*going awry*) Try and stop me... Early in the day, mind. You know the position I'm in... Pass on my congratulations to ... er... Give him my best anyway...

The music is now a loud cacophony

Edith? Edith?

But Edith has gone. Troop is living a nightmare. He tears the hat from his head and puts his hands over his ears in an attempt to shut out discord

Troop runs into the wings calling "Edith"

Music builds to a crescendo. The Lights flash. Total confusion

Then Troop in shirt and slacks bursts into the dressing-room

Music stops abruptly. The Lights go on around the mirror

(In total anguish) JESSIE!

Immediate light change, bulbs out round the dressing-table

Troop is an old man again, heartbroken, helpless and pathetic

Stephanie enters the dressing-room with his dressing-gown

Stephanie Hey, hey... *(offering the dressing-gown)* C'mon, let's get you into this.

Stephanie helps Troop into the dressing-gown as the Light grows on the sitting-room. She leads him gently into the sitting-room, soothing him as she goes

Troop I'm sorry...

Stephanie gently eases him into his chair

I'm a trial to you...
Stephanie No... You've helped me, Mr Troop.
Troop I know apology's not persuasion but you and me have been close. I've told you things.
Stephanie Told you a few things an' all.
Troop But I don't want you to turn your back. As bad as it's been you must follow your heart and not your head... You're a good girl. Remember, won't you? When the time comes?
Stephanie Yeah. *(She sorts Troop's cushions)* He came last night, did I tell you?
Troop Eh?
Stephanie My husband. Wants me to take him back... Doesn't do to hate, does it? You can spend a lifetime regretting... It means I'm leaving.
Troop *(taking this on board)* Ay... Ay, well the kiddie'll need you now.
Stephanie Matron wants to give me a bit of a send-off. You know, when we have the party.

Act II

Pause as she looks at Troop

    Am I being stupid?
Troop No ... no... Stay with the light.

Stephanie kisses Troop quickly and exits L

    (*To himself*) And them that love you for yourself...

Music Cue No 30

Troop dozes, still and deserted. Then gradually the Light and music change. Troop doesn't move throughout. Then the Light grows on Troop. Bird song

Edith enters L. *She carries a shopping bag*

She pauses to look a moment at sleeping Troop

Edith Hallo, Dad.

Troop rouses. Surprised at seeing her

Troop (*to Edith*) And what brings you to this knacker's yard?
Edith Well not the prospect of another row. Sorry if that disappoints you. (*She puts the bag down and sits on the chair*) Stephanie's party looks like fun. Balloons on the main gate, streamers round the door.

Troop broods

    Made herself very popular in the short time she's been here.

No response from Troop

    You and she have become good friends, haven't you?
Troop Eh?
Edith Stephanie.
Troop Stephanie? Which one's she?
Edith Come off it, Dad.

Stephanie enters quickly L

Stephanie Oh, hallo... You made it then?
Edith (*to Stephanie with the bag*) Cakes and wine are in here. (*She removes*

a camera from the bag) Oh, and I've brought my video camera. Capture the highlights.
Stephanie (*taking the bag*) Great!
Edith Matron will allow wine, won't she? Don't want to embarrass anybody.
Stephanie No problem. Can't get 'em legless, can we? Most of 'em can't walk anyway.

Edith and Stephanie laugh

Troop (*irate*) Show some bloody respect, damn yer! Old isn't an alien species, y'know. It's youth, without the optimism! All the way from Staines to a bloody do for someone you don't know. Should be ashamed.
Stephanie (*to Edith*) Sorry... Anyway ... got a party to get ready. See you later.

Stephanie exits L

Edith puts the bag on the table as Troop broods

Edith She's been good for you.
Troop Ay ... well, I was always better with strangers. Just family I failed to impress.
Edith I'm sure I'd be impressed if I knew. The boys are interested too but what can I tell them? All I know is that my father used to be on the stage.
Troop You can't kid a kidder. I gave up because you made me give up.
Edith That's your story, Dad.
Troop Haunted me till the guilt all but choked me. All justified, I'm not arguing.
Edith If you'd drop this persecution mania for just a second you might learn something.
Troop You put me in here.
Edith As much for your sake as for mine. I know you don't think much of me as a daughter but I had a family to consider. Anyway, this place has the time and facilities to give you the care you deserve... And the dignity. (*She sits resigned, her back to Troop*) Always nice to mention dignity when talking of old people. If I've walked about in your head, Dad, you've walked about in mine, believe me.
Troop Ay ... well... I was never easy. Your mother'd tell you that, God rest her... The frustration of failure.
Edith (*turning to Troop*) You topped the bill.

Troop makes a dismissive gesture

Oh you did, that's a fact... I'm sorry I never saw you perform.

Act II

Troop Didn't miss much.
Edith I think I did.

An awkward pause

Stephanie enters quickly, excited. She wears a party hat and has streamers round her neck

Stephanie Edith! Bring your camera. (*To Troop*) Great news! The illusionist is coming after all. Got this terrific idea... He puts me in the cabinet and I say "tarrah" as he draws the drapes. When he opens them again I've gone.
Troop Jesus!
Stephanie (*to Edith*) What d'yer think?
Edith I think it sounds wonderful. (*She picks up her bag*)

Stephanie and Edith exit L

Troop (*loudly towards exit* L) Wonderful? It's bloody diabolical! (*He struggles upright*) Might be a fart-arse old folks' home but you're committing the unforgivable... (*He shuffles unwittingly to the opened piano*) You never top a bill with a speciality act! Never!

He sits down and looks for a moment at the keys. He plays a few tentative notes. Then more confidently into Waltz Around the Floor

Music Cue No 31. *Midway through, as music takes up the theme, he rises and goes to the chair for his stick*

(*Loudly towards exit* L) I'll follow the illusionist... Tell 'em to hang on to their zimmer frames... Harry Troop's back! (*He shuffles towards exit* L *twirling his stick*)

Music continues as Troop exits

CURTAIN

FURNITURE AND PROPERTY LIST

Further dressing may be added at the director's discretion

ACT I

On stage: SITTING-ROOM SETTING:
2 odd armchairs
Settee
Small table
Upright piano
Screen
Transportable pay phone
Wheelchair
Walking stick
Papers
Magazines
Scatter cushions
Mirror

DRESSING-ROOM SETTING:
Dressing mirror surrounded by bulbs
Make-up
Dressing-table. *In drawer:* contract
Picture wrapped in brown paper
Trunk
Footstool

Off stage: Mug of tea, duster, polish (**Stephanie**)
Walking stick (**Troop**)
Straw hat, clip dickie-bow (**Troop**)
Shopping bag containing detective books, fruit, scrapbook with things attached (**Edith**)
Spectacles (**Troop**)
Towel (**Stella**)
Suitcase (**Stella**)
Cigarettes, lighter (**Troop**)

Furniture and Property List 71

Personal: **Troop:** monocle, straw hat
Stephanie: coins, cigarettes, lighter
Troop: watch (worn throughout)

ACT II

Set: Hoover
Scrapbook in piano
Bottle of beer
Glasses

Off stage: Spectacles (**Troop**)
Rose (**Jessie**)
Vase of flowers, radio cassette player (**Stephanie**)
Night-light in jam jar (**Jessie**)
Shopping bag containing cakes, wine bottles, camera (**Edith**)
Clipboard with script, old BBC stand microphone (**BBC Woman**)
Rifle (**Troop**)
Rifle (**Jessie**)
Party hat, streamers (**Stephanie**)

Personal: **Stephanie:** piece of paper
BBC Woman: horn-rimmed spectacles, headphones
Troop: coins
Jessie: watch
Stephanie: cigarette

LIGHTING PLOT

Property fittings required: bulbs round dressing-room mirror
1 interior. The same throughout

ACT I

To open: Dark stage

Cue 1	Laughter fades to silence *After a pause, bring up spot on* **Troop**	(Page 1)
Cue 2	**Troop** takes a bow *Black-out; then bring up lights on sitting-room*	(Page 3)
Cue 3	**Troop**: "I'll not die a nobody!" *Fade lights down slightly*	(Page 11)
Cue 4	**Stella**: "…to see us any time at all." *Reduce lighting*	(Page 20)
Cue 5	**Troop** exits *Black-out; then gradually bring up lights*	(Page 20)
Cue 6	**Stella**: "Six months, then we'll think again." *Black-out; then bring up spot* DS, *twinkling showtime* *lights along footlights and around proscenium*	(Page 21)
Cue 7	**Troop**: "…darling partner, Miss Stella Turner!" *Bring up spot on* **Stella**	(Page 21)
Cue 8	**Troop** and **Stella** exit *Black-out*	(Page 24)
Cue 9	*Soulmates* is played softly, reduced in tempo *Bring up lights on sitting-room*	(Page 24)
Cue 10	**Troop**: "How best to catch the light." *Brighten lights, snap on bulb surround on mirror*	(Page 29)

Lighting Plot 73

| Cue 11 | **Troop** throws picture at the wall
Black-out | (Page 36) |

ACT II

To open:	Overall lighting on sitting-room	
Cue 12	**Stephanie** exits with sweeper *Fade sitting-room lights*	(Page 45)
Cue 13	**Troop** bounds into dressing-room area *Cross-fade to dressing-room area*	(Page 45)
Cue 14	**Troop**: "Jessie!" *Black-out*	(Page 47)
Cue 15	*Wedding March* is played *Bring up spot on* **Jessie** *and* **Troop**	(Page 48)
Cue 16	**Jessie** stands on prostrate **Troop** *Black-out*	(Page 48)
Cue 17	**Troop** hugs **Jessie** affectionately *Cross-fade to sitting-room*	(Page 48)
Cue 18	**Stephanie** goes off after **Troop** *Cross-fade to general lighting*	(Page 52)
Cue 19	**Troop** plays the audience *Spotlight follows him*	(Page 55)
Cue 20	**Troop**: "...the lodger's getting on top of her!" *Black-out; then bring up lights on sitting-room*	(Page 55)
Cue 21	**Stephanie** exits after **Troop** *Fade lights down on sitting-room*	(Page 58)
Cue 22	Air-raid siren is heard *Searchlight scans stage and audience*	(Page 58)
Cue 23	**Jessie** comes on with a night-light *Snap off searchlight*	(Page 58)

Cue 24	**Jessie**: "How d'you feel?" *Bring up general lighting*	(Page 59)
Cue 25	**Troop** and **Jessie** salute *Black-out; then slowly bring up lights on sitting-room*	(Page 61)
Cue 26	**Troop**: "Why didn't she tell me?" *Slowly dim light on* **Troop** *and* **Stephanie**	(Page 63)
Cue 27	**Troop** exits *Bring up lights on stage wings*	(Page 63)
Cue 28	**Troop** is having difficulty stepping *Flash lights, continuing*	(Page 65)
Cue 29	Music stops abruptly *Stop flashing, snap on mirror lights*	(Page 66)
Cue 30	**Troop**: "Jessie!" *Change lighting abruptly, snap off mirror bulbs*	(Page 66)
Cue 31	**Stephanie** helps **Troop** into dressing-gown *Bring up lights on sitting-room*	(Page 66)
Cue 32	**Troop** dozes *Gradually change lighting, then brighten on* **Troop**	(Page 67)

EFFECTS PLOT

ACT I

Cue 1 To open Act I (Page 1)
Fade up seaside sounds—seagulls crying; mix with audience laughter, then fade up laughter above fading seaside sounds. Hold laughter a moment. Fade laughter to silence

ACT II

Cue 2 **Stephanie** assists **Troop** to sit in chair (Page 42)
Phone rings

Cue 3 **Stephanie**: "Too late for that... I'll kill that Mandy." (Page 42)
Sound of OAPs singing Daisy in lounge off

Cue 4 **Stephanie** exits (Page 42)
Cut singing

Cue 5 Black-out (Page 47)
Wedding bells

Cue 6 **Troop**: "Any daughter would be proud." (Page 51)
Phone rings

Cue 7 **BBC Woman**: "All set are we?" (Page 52)
Static whine

Cue 8 **Stephanie** sits on stool (Page 56)
Toby on tape as script page 56

Cue 9 **Stephanie**: "It's Gramps." (Page 57)
Ben on tape as script page 57

Cue 10 **Troop** sits distracted (Page 57)
Dialogue and sounds on tape as script page 57

Cue 11	**Troop** drops the player *Cut tape sounds*	(Page 58)
Cue 12	Lights go down on sitting-room *Air-raid siren, continuing*	(Page 58)
Cue 13	Searchlight goes off *Fade siren off*	(Page 58)
Cue 14	**Troop** soft-shoes *Waltz Around the Floor* reprise **Little Edith** *on tape as script page 65*	(Page 65)
Cue 15	**Troop**: "What is it, pet?" **Little Edith** *on tape as script page 65*	(Page 65)
Cue 16	**Troop**: "Nanna Lester looking after you, is she?" **Little Edith** *on tape as script page 65*	(Page 65)
Cue 17	**Troop**: "Don't worry." **Little Edith** *on tape as script page 65*	(Page 65)
Cue 18	**Troop** dances on **Edith** *on tape as script page 65*	(Page 65)
Cue 19	**Troop**: "Do I know him?" **Edith** *on tape as script page 65*	(Page 65)
Cue 20	**Troop**: "My turn'll come." **Edith** *on tape as script page 65*	(Page 65)
Cue 21	**Troop**: "Height of the season." **Edith** *on tape as script page 65*	(Page 65)
Cue 22	Light grows on **Troop** *Bird song*	(Page 67)